THE 5 SENTENCE METHOD

HOW TO WRITE YOUR DAMN BOOK, ALREADY.

REBECCA THORNE

THE 5 SENTENCE METHOD

HOW TO WRITE YOUR DAMN BOOK, ALREADY.

Copyright @ 2023 Rebecca Thorne

For permissions, contact: *rebeccathornewrites@gmail.com*

Cover Design by Rebecca Thorne

Dragon Design by Anna Oman
https://www.instagram.com/ohjeezoman/

ISBN 978-1-962597-01-2 (*print edition*)
ISBN 978-1-962597-00-5 (*ebook*)

1 2 3 4 5 6 7 8 9 10

www.rebeccathorne.net

For the authors: the intrepid, the nervous, the excited.

You are more courageous than you realize.

You can do this.

CONTENTS

ONE

SO, YOU WANT TO WRITE A BOOK?

FIRST OFF, fuck yeah. Nice job! We're all about that energy here.

No, truly. A 2021 survey of 2000 United States respondents revealed that "15 percent have actually started writing a book," and a mere "six percent" had reached the halfway point of their novels. [1] Which basically means, just by buying this book, you *rock.*

While the rest of the world spends their time *thinking* about writing, you're taking steps to do it. Maybe you're just conceptualizing your book right now, and want to learn how to properly approach the novel-writing process. Maybe you've already started writing a novel, and got stuck. Or maybe you're finished with your book (hell YES, awesome work), and are paralyzed in fear at the concept of editing.

Don't worry, don't fret. Shake off that paralysis.

I've got you.

My name is Rebecca Thorne, and I'm an author of fantasy, science fiction, and romance. Most of my books lean into the LGBTQIA+ spectrum, and I'm most known for my bestselling cozy fantasy novel *Can't Spell Treason Without Tea*. I'm also responsible for the *This Gilded Abyss* trilogy and the hit contemporary fantasy *The Day Death Stopped*.

Basically, I write a *lot*. Which means I've probably made all the mistakes you're hoping to avoid, and read all the craft books you're contemplating purchasing.

So, why this book? Why am I qualified to teach you how to draft a novel quickly, easily, and efficiently?

Cue my ad-nauseam list of credentials:

- I spent a decade in this business—eight years in traditional publishing, and two in indie publishing.
- I have books both self-published and traditionally published.
- I've sold over 20,000 copies of my books.
- My cozy fantasy series (originally self-published) was sold to Tor UK and Bramble (Tor US) in a significant deal.
- I earned a Master of Fine Arts in Popular Fiction Writing and Publishing from Emerson College. I was also chosen as the commencement speaker for graduation.

- I maintain a TikTok presence of over 35,000 followers (as of November 2023), and spend plenty of time on platforms like Instagram, Threads, BlueSky, and Discord.
- I've developed and taught private writing courses across multiple platforms.
- I'm deeply engrained in many writing communities, so I talk to other writers about this stuff. I'm a nerd, and I think plot structure is fascinating.

Point is, I've spent *years* experimenting with every single plotting style I could find. I've played around with every piece of advice. I've challenged myself to test out dozens of genres. I've literally done it all for you, so that *you* can learn quickly, then get to what's most important: writing your damn book.

Will this craft book be able to write your novel for you? No, not at all. You're going to have to put in the time, energy, and work to make this happen. There's a reason only six percent of folks got *halfway* through their books. It's hard.

But knowledge makes it easier.

I'm going to split this book into multiple, easy-to-read sections so that you can skim and jump around as needed. While I do recommend reading it in order, you can technically skip to any part of this book as time allows. The only part of this book that builds on itself is Chapter 3 and Chapter 4. Everything else? Go ham.

Let's plot your book, shall we?

PLOTTER OR PANTSER?

Apparently, most authors fall in one of two categories. They're either a "pantser" or a "plotter."

Pantsers write by the seat of their pants. They live by that E.L. Doctorow quote: *"Writing a novel is like driving a car at night. You never see further than your headlights, but you can make the whole trip that way."* The thrill comes from discovering what's next in the same breath as their characters. Basically, they're all vibes, no plan.

Plotters, meanwhile, are *only* plans. They usually keep meticulous character sheets and reference outlines that can top 10,000 words (or more!). Their worldbuilding will span centuries. Their creativity is best while they're recording ideas; by the time they sit down to write the book, they've already had those revelations and exciting moments of discovery. After that, it's just a matter of putting pen to paper.

Plotters scare me.

Pantsers scare me too, now, but for an entirely different reason. I spent years in the "pantser" camp. I felt that outlines were the death of my creativity, and that my best writing came when I had no idea what was happening.

Need more excitement? Add an explosion. Not sure why she's breaking up with him? Maybe he's a ghost. My best plot twists came from diving so deep into my novel that I'd gasp whenever I surfaced. It was exhilarating.

But, *boy*, the revision process *sucked*.

Pantsing worked so well for me when I just... didn't edit. Why bother fixing a story? Obviously, it was perfect the first time. But once I moved into desiring publication, I realized that mindset wouldn't get me far.

Editing is a necessity. Period.

So, I started hunting for ways to make it easier, and that's when I realized there's a whole group of people plotters and pantsers don't encompass.

SECRET OPTION THREE: PLANTSERS!

I think the 5 Sentence Method will appeal to a very specific audience: the authors who don't identify as a plotter or a pantser... or maybe they do, but they aren't happy about it.

Pantsing exclusively delayed my publication career by years. If I'd learned plot structure and gotten *something* on paper before I started writing, my books would have been so much better, so much faster.

Thus, this book, so you can get a lot better than me, hopefully faster than I figured this shit out.

The 5 Sentence Method is for us plantsers. The writers who want to plot, but aren't sure how to start. Those of you who still want to be surprised by their novel sometimes, but without extensive edits once the book is finished.

You want to know the plot is on track while still discovering the heart of your book over the journey.

If you nodded along to that, this is your craft book.

The 5 Sentence Method is simple. It's fast. And it allows for the pantser in me to experience that thrill of discovery while appeasing the part of me that desperately wants to be a plotter.

BEFORE WE BEGIN, LET'S TALK ABOUT PUBLISHING.

This book is for people who want to become better writers, and I assume most of you have the end-goal of publication.

I feel you! At first, I was happy just writing my books, and there's no shame in that. High school and college Rebecca spent her time writing anything she wanted, and delighted in handing cheaply bound copies out to her friends and family. If you're at this stage, that's A-OK, and you'll still enjoy reading about writing, I'm sure.

But things change when you decide to pursue publication.

I was in my early twenties when I made the shift, and immediately, I was smacked with a hard truth.

PUBLISHING IS A BUSINESS.

Read that as many times as you need. It's the most important lesson in this book.

Writing is a creative art. But the minute you decide to publish, you are entering a professional industry, where sales speak loudest and gatekeepers are rampant.

Agents don't give two shits if that end-of-book plot twist will blow their socks off. If they can't make it past page one, or ten, or 50, they *will never see it.*

Industry professionals are so inundated with books that they are looking for reasons to stop reading yours.

Do not give them that reason.

If your goal is to publish—or even just write something readers will love—you *have* to learn about plot structure. Because the business of publishing expects something very different than your best friend or your mother. Once you decide to pursue publication, you aren't writing for yourself anymore... and your readers have demands.

LEARN FROM MY MISTAKES.

Between 2014 - 2018, I queried three novels. I didn't get a single full request for the first two. I did, however, amass 300+ rejections over those years.

You know what finally snagged my first literary agent?

Editing my fucking book.

Learning how to write, learning what was expected—that was my deep dive of 2016 - 2018. I read every craft book I could find. I explored every plot structure on the internet. To this day, my craft bookshelf is used frequently.

I learned what my readers—and by extension, these agents—were expecting. And only then did I succeed.

(Relatively speaking, anyway. Publishing is still a rough business that relies heavily on luck, but that's for another craft book.)

Don't waste years tossing good books at a wall, hoping one will stick. Instead, learn about plot structure and the craft of writing, and *edit* that book until good becomes *great*.

Trust me. Your future self will thank you.

TWO
VITAL QUESTIONS TO ASK BEFORE WRITING

BEFORE WE START PLOTTING your new book, there are seven questions I'd like you to answer. That's the point of Chapter 2.

These things are important, and if you aren't thinking about them early, I guarantee it'll bite you in the ass when the book is finished. But, as always, you are free to skip this chapter if you'd like to get to another topic.

Still, if you have the time, please come back and reference this section. I promise it's worth your while.

QUESTION 1: HOW ARE YOU GOING TO PUBLISH?

Some of you may not want to publish your book at all... and if so, this section is *not* for you. Skip it. Or read it, and keep it in mind for the future!

For anyone sticking around, we should review the two current paths to publication: traditional publishing and self-publishing.

I'll make a brief note at the end about hybrid publishing, which is a combination of the two, and small press publishing, which almost overlaps with self-publishing.

But for now, just assume there are two paths to success. **Neither is better than the other.** As someone who's done both, trust me on this. Some authors will do better in traditional publishing, and some in self-publishing. It's a *personal preference*, nothing more.

I'm planning to write an entirely separate craft book on publishing paths, so if this interests you, check out my Amazon page around December 2024.

For now, let's simplify these paths.

TRADITIONAL PUBLISHING

Traditional Publishing (or "trad pub") is the path of obtaining a literary agent to represent your book and career.

This literary agent will proceed to send your novel to editors at various publishing houses (ideally, the Big 5, which is an industry term for the biggest publishers: Simon & Schuster, Hachette, Penguin/Random House, Macmillan, and Harper Collins). Each of these publishing houses has dozens of "imprints," which are basically smaller publishing houses inside the big, umbrella publisher. If an editor at an imprint likes your book, they buy it. (It's a lot more complex, but again, I'll save that run-down for a future book.)

If your book is bought, cue the expectation of fame: book tours, merch, big figure advances, etc.

None of this is guaranteed—and *every* traditional publishing deal, even mine, required a huge element of luck—but this is the ideal, gold standard of traditional publishing. This is what every trad author hopes to achieve.

Self-Publishing

Self-publishing (AKA: "self pub" or "indie publishing") is the process of publishing your novel yourself. You may distribute through a wholesaler like Amazon or Ingram Spark, but you're doing all the back-end work yourself. Cover design, interior formatting, marketing, editing... you're in charge of all of it, which means you have unlimited control. It also means you bear all of the expenses.

The process to self-publish looks different for every author. Some prefer to sell directly to readers via their website. Some prefer to list a book on Amazon and just collect a paycheck. The hallmarks of indie authors, though, is full control and a faster paycheck. Where it might take years to be paid in trad pub, indie authors can earn royalties in 60 days or less.

Again, **neither option is bad.** It ultimately just depends on your preference. If you want the possibility of a big advance + a team working for your novel, trad pub is your goal. If you want to do it yourself and get the book out there, and enjoy a paycheck this year, self-pub is your goal.

A Note **on Small Press Publishing**

There is a smaller subsect of self-publishing, where you submit without a literary agent to a small press. I personally do not recommend this path. Anyone can call themselves a "press," and publish books, but they're using the same channels as true self-pubbed authors are. This means you lose your book rights and a substantial amount of your royalties for a distributor that can't extend further than if you'd handled it alone.

In addition, many small presses—through ignorance, malice, or both—take advantage of new authors. They say "yes" to your book, which is a rarity in this industry, and often present a contract riddled with predatory clauses. Since new authors don't know any better, so they sign on the dotted line.

If a small press is interested in your book, always double-check with their other authors before signing anything. Ask how their experience with this press was. See if you like where their books ended up—are they in bookstores, or just available on Amazon? In my experience, authors who sign with small presses often regret that call later.)

Hybrid Publishing

The final option for you is what my path is: a hybrid path. Basically, someone who does both self-publishing *and* traditional publishing.

This is my personal path. I started in trad pub, switched to indie, and now do both simultaneously. For me, this meant my self-published series was bought by a Big 5 publisher (Macmillan distributes Tor's books). I also still self-publish, and my literary agent focuses on selling those rights abroad.

Hybrid paths are trickier to achieve, but can be done. Still, for new authors, I recommend choosing self-publishing or traditional publishing. Once you choose, don't be afraid to swap to the other side if you feel it fits you better!

When choosing a publication path, there is no wrong answer, and you are free to change your mind.

How your publication **path affects your book:**

The fact is that self-published authors have more flexibility with their book's content.

Traditionally published authors—or authors hoping to be trad pubbed—need to think on a business level. You're trying to woo *huge* corporations... and they won't spend money on something that isn't proven to work. Which means, for trad authors, you will need to focus on bestsellers in your genre, find "comparable" or "comp" titles (books similar to your novel that performed well *recently*, not a decade ago), and lean into how your book will fit alongside them on a shelf.

Indie authors, meanwhile, only need to cater to their readers. I always cite the example of massive bestseller *Legends & Lattes*, by NYT Bestseller Travis Baldree. He essentially coined the "cozy fantasy" subgenre with this novel—but he self-published it first. If he'd tried to traditionally publish it, I bet he'd have been rejected over and over, because trad pub books in the past favored high stakes... and his book did not.

By self-publishing *Legends & Lattes*, he was able to grab an entire group of readers the Big 5 publishers were ignoring: the readers who wanted quieter fantasy with lower stakes. And after he struck gold, these publishers spent 2023 scrambling to acquire their own cozy fantasy lists.

With all of this in mind, ask yourself:

- What genre is my book?
- Are there successful, mainstream books like it?
  (IE: can you walk into Barnes & Noble and find a book similar to yours?)

- Can I twist my idea into something that would be perceived as more "commercial"? (IE: how vampires were hot hot hot after *Twilight*, and how dystopian soared after *Hunger Games*? Right now, we're entering the era of dragons, thanks to *Fourth Wing*.)

Keep those answers in the back of your head as you're plotting your book. Your publication path *will* matter later on.

QUESTION 2: WHAT'S YOUR HOOK?

Remember how I said that every novel follows the same structure... the bones? Well, it's time to talk about the muscle, skin, and features of your unique novel.

Let's chat about your "hook."

In simplistic terms, the hook is a literary technique used to grab readers fast. Ideally, it piques their interest before they even pick up the book.

It could be a genre-bending trait, like *Gideon the Ninth*'s famous "Lesbian Necromancers in Space" cover quote. It could be a twist on something new, like the creative writing style in *Good Omens* (omniscient narration, footnotes, personification of items, etc). Or it could be a unique "what if" question that leaves readers wondering (IE: "What if whales existed in the vacuum of space?")

Point is, there are a lot of hooks in the world. But condensing yours into a few words is ideal—and pulling on that hook throughout the writing process will keep your book feeling fresh and unique.

So, in one sentence, what is your hook? Why should readers drop *everything* to block off hours of their valuable time and consume your novel? What will keep them frothing at the mouth, hoping for more?

Now, add dragons. Because everything is better with dragons.

That's ~~mostly~~ a joke.

QUESTION 3: WHAT IS YOUR BOOK'S GENRE?

I actually hate genres. I hate the idea of codifying books into "neat" categories that actually become very messy when you dive into them. But unfortunately, businesses need categories to know how things are selling, and consumers (readers) need them to know what they like. And thus, we wind up with genres.

In Emerson College, I took a graduate course that focused on "genre blending." We read books like *A Master of Djinn* and *This is How You Lose the Time War*, and we debated genres fiercely. The consensus at the course's end was that books like these straddled many genre lines.

Nothing was simplistic.

"It's undefinable" works for some people, and might work for you. However, I will offer a word of caution, especially for anyone planning to pursue traditional publishing: you're going to need comparable titles. If you straddle too many genres, finding comps will be very, very hard.

Before my genre blending course, I took another class on marketing. The professor—a long-time industry professional with the Big 5—only taught a few courses, and during our semester he accepted a job to run acquisitions at Disney Press.

He gave us an assignment: go to Barnes & Noble, and find the *physical shelf* that your book fits on.

Because that's the crux of publishing, isn't it? Especially in the trad pub spheres, books won't sell if they aren't neatly classified. When a bookseller gets their hands on your novel, they need to know where to *put* it inside their store.

Fantasy? Science fiction? Romance?

Or maybe just the #BookTok table, which is quickly becoming a catch-all for the viral novels booktokkers are growing to love.

I want to emphasize: choosing one genre is not a hard and fast rule. You can blatantly ignore everything in this book if you'd like. Break all the rules; most of them suck anyway.

But publishing is competitive as shit... and in traditional publishing, an agent is looking for two things:

- Do they love it?
- Will it sell?

If the answer isn't an emphatic, easy "yes!!" to either of those, an agent will pass. And that doesn't mean your book is bad. It just means that **publishing is a business**, and "commercial success" exists for a reason. Popular books are widely accessible to the general public. It's psychologically expected that your book will have a genre, because that is what society has conditioned us to want.

Even for self-published authors, this is important, because your genre depicts your comparable titles. Those books, the ones "like" yours, will be your guiding star in choosing a cover design, interior formatting, book size, book length, etc. Your readers have probably already read those fabulously popular comp titles. By framing your book to match—cover, tropes, description, etc—your book will be on the tip of readers' tongues when someone hunts for a similar novel.

Did I mention publishing is a business?

Yeah. I know.

Remember your genre, because we're going to be discussing word count lengths later on. It's going to come in handy. Trust me.

QUESTION 4: WHY THAT MAIN CHARACTER?

This might seem stupid, but you *have* to answer this question before you start plotting. What about your MC deserves an entire book? Why follow this person and not someone else?

Failing to think critically about this could result in a side character swooping in later to steal the show... and that will result in a *massive* rewrite, I promise you.

Let's work smart, not hard. Time to dive into what makes a great MC.

There are dozens of craft books on character, and all of them have different qualifications for creating a character that feels real. Expert craft writer Jeff Gerke (*First 50 Pages, Plot vs Character,* and others) stated that your MC should fall into one of these five personality traits:

- Heroic - brave, selfless, willing to help
- Principled - abiding by a strict code to better humanity
- Sympathetic - the underdog who still has hope for the future

- Winsome - charming and delightful, someone we love to follow
- Smart - able to outthink the competition

Save the Cat (Blake Snyder), meanwhile, proffers the belief that you can have the douchiest MC ever, but if they help / save an animal, a child, or an elderly person, we will like them by nature. (I challenge you to examine your favorite movies, and see how *often* Hollywood uses this technique.)

The point is, your main character has to be the *most*. If they're sympathetic, they need to be the most sympathetic person in your novel. If they're brave, they'd better be braver than anyone, even in the face of their fear. If they're charming, no one should be stealing their spotlight in any situation.

Okay, you have your MC. You're confident they're the one. Awesome! Next thing to consider:

What is their flaw?

And no, it shouldn't be that they're too clumsy or perfect.

Jeff Gerke is one of my favorite craft writers, and he calls this the "knot"—something that disrupts the rope of the MC, something they have to unravel in their soul before they can succeed. A good plot always, always pits the MC against their fatal flaw somehow. In the end, this shortcoming will bite them in the ass.

And if they can't overcome it, people will die—metaphorically or literally, depending on genre.

You have a ton of flexibility to determine your MC's flaw, so get creative. We'll be talking about theme in a minute, but your MC's flaw is a great way to sneakily discuss your theme.

To amplify a character's personality, consider contrasting traits.

Another way to add depth to your character with ease is by adding a contrasting trait. Say you're following the head cheerleader stereotype. Well... what if she dreams of being a mechanic, and spends every spare minute under cars? How would a girl unafraid of grease, oil, and grime fit in with the carefully manicured queens of school?

In this case, her flaw might be recognizing that she's allowed to be two things—and that one doesn't necessarily negate the other. But that will be a long journey of growth for our prom queen, I'm sure.

Basically, take a caricature, and add a contrasting trait... and you've probably just created someone very interesting.

A BRIEF aside about personality quizzes:

Many authors love using personality quizzes to compartmentalize their characters, and this is honestly great brainstorming! If you're working on a character profile, I think personality quizzes can be a big help.

But I always offer a word of caution: make sure you remember the *environmental impact* on these personality types. For example, a logical, factual MC will act very different if they're facing an alien invasion versus struggling to obtain tenure.

No personality test will ever go that in-depth, so it's your job to get in the head of your MC with these facets in mind. Think of it like an image with different filters: same picture, very different tones depending on the genre.

QUESTION 5: WHO IS YOUR VILLAIN?

When I attended DFWCon back in 2017, they had a theme to the conference: heroes versus villains. Authors picked sides, then argued their case about why their side was superior.

I picked villains, because I believe villains are the most important part of your story. We won that conference debate because no one could argue with us.

Villains are the beating heart of your book.

Full stop.

Until a *true* villain surfaces in your book, your MC will go unchallenged. Even the most heroic MC will be twiddling their thumbs until a villain fucks something up. The plot literally cannot start without them or some ripple effect action they've caused.

Now, villains don't have to be people. They can be concepts, like fate or luck, or something unsurmountable like a society or nature itself. So, let's simplify things for ease of access:

A villain is someone with <u>an opposing goal</u> to the main character.

That's it. It's truly that simple.

Your villain is whoever (or whatever) wants to *stop* your MC from getting what they want, or feel they need. This doesn't mean your villain is the "bad guy." Most of the time, they're just someone who presents an alternate argument to the world at large.

If your MC's goal is survival, your villain is trying to kill them. It might not be personal, but that's the crux of the conflict. In *The Hunger Games*, this manifests in multiple villains, but the true one is the Capitol, and by extension President Snow.

If your MC's goal is love, your villain wants them loveless. In a movie like *The Proposal*, there are token villains, but the true villain is the MC herself—and how she's actively sabotaging the single relationship she has.

Les Miserables has one of the greatest villains of all time, in my mind. Javier is a police officer—a "principled" MC, if the story were told from his perspective—who abides by a strict code of ethics. And our actual hero, Jean Valjean, challenges those ethics every single time they meet. By the end, Javier simply cannot accept this new world view, because he realizes that abiding by this "code" has made him a villain... and he spent the entire story thinking he was the hero. It literally gives me chills.

The final example is the movie *Megamind*. Metroman (the hero) becomes Megamind's villain, simply because he retires and Megamind isn't ready to accept that. Again, there are token side villains, but the biggest conflict happened inside Megamind's own soul as a direct result of Metroman leaving the business.

As I said above, villains do not have to be evil. They just have to want something your MC doesn't... and they need to be powerful enough to obtain their goals if the MC doesn't intervene.

Truly synergetic villains are the opposite side of a coin to your MC. Often, one single moment will set your hero and villain on opposite paths—but they'll always be running parallel to each other.

**If circumstances were different,
your villain could *be* your main character.**

Villains are awesome. Always give yours the attention they deserve.

QUESTION 6: WHAT'S YOUR THEME?

Themes can seem simple on the surface, but they're influencing the entire undercurrent of your novel—which means you need to think critically about what you're trying to *say* with this book.

There's an ongoing discussion in the writer world about what makes a theme. Is it a simple concept, like "love" or "success"? Or is it closer to your story's looming question, like, "will she find love?" or "will that job bring success?"

I personally think theme is a bit simpler.

**For this craft book's purposes,
your theme is your central argument.**

Themes are you, the author, speaking to the reader through your characters and their actions. It's you, asserting your worldview in an argument of fictional rhetoric.

Imagine you're a member of a debate team, and you've been handed a topic—like love, war, oppression, the pursuit of happiness, or a dozen other things. Lucky you, you already have an opinion. Now it's time to argue your point—that love is great, that war is terrible, that oppression should be stopped, that happiness can be found anywhere.

Your reader, meanwhile, is waiting to be convinced of that fact. Some might be more skeptical and take a bit more persuasion, but they're at least willing to hear you out.

What, exactly, are you going to tell them?

That argument is your theme. Keep it in the back of your brain as you plot and write your novel, because it should influence everything that happens from here on out. Make your statement, and make it loudly through your characters' actions.

THEME EXAMPLES

Here are some theme examples, pulled from some Pixar movies we're going to explore later (screenplays are perhaps the greatest examples of tight writing, and old-school Pixar was the king). I've added some summaries in case you haven't seen these movies, too!

- *Up* – A grieving man recovers from his beloved wife's death through the adventure they never took together. (**Theme:** It's okay to move on from a loss.)
- *Wall-E* – The last robot on a decimated Earth finds a living plant, and has to recall humanity.

(**Theme**: Hope can be found in very unlikely places, if only you stop and look.)
- *Finding Nemo* – An overly-protective father fish has to rescue his captured son. (**Theme**: The greatest strength comes from letting go.)
- *The Incredibles* – A washed-up superhero must learn to incorporate his family in his old business. (**Theme**: Family is stronger together than one man is alone.)

Start analyzing the themes from your favorite movies or books! See if you notice any that resonate.

QUESTION 7: WHY ARE YOU THE BEST AUTHOR FOR THIS STORY?

This final question separates the bad writers from the great ones. It's uncomfortable, and makes people bristle in defense, but it *has to be asked*.

<u>Why are you the best author to write this book?</u>

We're all familiar with authors being "canceled" online. Believe it or not, it's become so prevalent in recent years that Big 5 publishing contracts include a clause about what happens if you're canceled. (Hint: this is one of the only ways you'd have to pay back an advance—if your novel creates a big enough outrage that they literally can't publish it anymore. It's *very* rare, but is written into some contracts.)

This scares people, and understandably so. Cancel culture is terrifying for most authors—trust me, you aren't alone in fearing it. However, I firmly believe that folks aren't canceled for no reason. In my experience, they're canceled because 1) the author didn't listen to marginalized people while trying to represent them, and 2) because the author didn't think *critically* about what they were putting into the world.

We no longer publish in an isolated ecosystem, one with zero reader contact once the book is released. If you are publishing, people will read your novel. You'll be expected to talk about it to crowds. And remember, your theme is your argument—so if you're arguing for terrible things, your readers are going to argue back.

And readers argue very, very loudly.

Some examples:

- If you are white, you likely do not have the experiences to write the Black experience.
- If you come from a lineage of colonizers, you are probably not the best voice for an oppressed race.
- If you are a straight woman, you are likely not the most accurate voice to portray a spicy book with two gay men.

This isn't meant to be mean. You have a book in your soul, and trust me, I get it. But if you are not actively engaging with folks in these communities—if you are not actively pursuing opinions outside your own—you likely haven't done the research to write these perspectives properly.

And sometimes, you can research for years and *still* not understand what it's like to be threatened for kissing your same-sex partner in public.

Everything you write is influenced by what you believe. That theme, right? That internal argument. You have opinions on how the world works, largely based in your own experiences of the world. Examining those experiences critically is an absolute necessity before you put pen to paper.

The end of Chapter 9 has a quick reference on resources for writing diversely, and a how-to guide on addressing cancel culture. Turns out, my career as a flight attendant actually did give me some pointers in handling customer outrage.

But those tips begins with this question, so please, *please* ask it of yourself.

Why are you the best author for this story?

If a reason doesn't immediately come to mind, the answer is probably: "I'm not."

THREE
MY INSPIRATION FOR THE 5 SENTENCE METHOD

OKAY, you've answered your questions, and you're armed with the basic knowledge you need to begin plotting your book! Fucking awesome!!

But before we dive into the 5 Sentence Method, I want to take a chapter and discuss inspiration for it.

FIRST, A DISCLAIMER.

As you're exploring this craft book, please remember: **nothing is created in a vacuum**.

I've spent a decade learning my craft—double that, if you count the years I was just writing for fun. Over that time, I've devoured so many craft books that I have entire bookshelf dedicated to them. Many of those books and websites are worth exploring—which is why I added a recommendations list to the back of this book.

The 5 Sentence Method draws heavy inspiration from the Three Act Structure and two other plotting methods: *My Story Can Beat Up Your Story* and the Snowflake Method.

Some authors, like K.M. Weiland, have done similar write-ups on "pinch points," which are basically a more in-depth version of the 5 Sentence Method. You can find K.M. Weiland's books in the resource section at the end of this novel!

After some Googling, there are a few authors with blogs about tying word counts to percentages. Mary Carroll Moore's website was the main one I found.[1] I found a mention of *Save the Cat*'s percentage points, but that book was waaay too in-depth for me, personally.

Point is, my inspiration came from all over.

When I first started talking about this method, I used claiming words: "*my* method," "this method *I* created," etc. I'd been using this method so long that I forgot to look critically at where it developed in my brain. That was insensitive, and I have since amended my language around it.

Just for clarity's sake: I'm not trying to claim ownership of the idea of tying five sentences to plot points. That's actually a very common plot structure, and I'm just one more author analyzing it.

I'm certain that the 5 Sentence Method existed in other iterations before I started using it.

To be honest, I just think it's cool! It's really helped me streamline my writing process, and I hope it can do the same for you.

As you dive into this method, don't forget that everyone learns differently. I always encourage new writers (and experienced ones!) to push themselves; try new plotting methods and adapt until something sticks.

The 5 Sentence Method is just *one* plotting option. I've listed several more throughout this craft book, and each are worth a look.

Let's explore a few!

THE THREE ACT STRUCTURE

We're going to talk a lot about psychology in this book.

Turns out, humans in the same areas learn the same rules. They may have variations, but these rules are largely influenced by our culture, ethnicities, and backgrounds. And Western readers are heavily swayed towards one specific plot:

The Three Act Structure.

We all remember this from our Shakespeare lessons, right? Looks something like this?

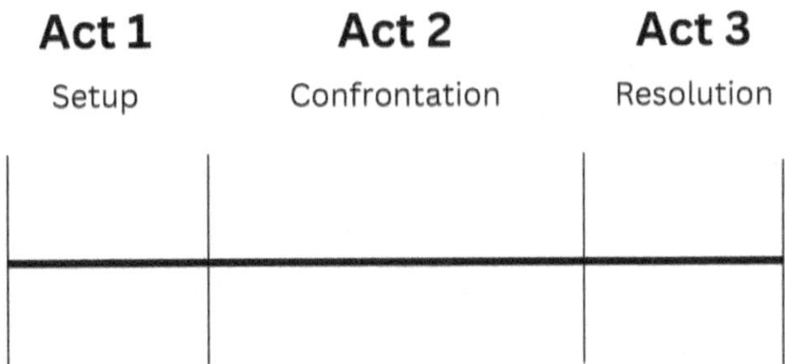

Three Act Structure

Popularized by Syd Field in:
Screenplay: The Foundations of Screenwriting

It says "popularized by" in that graphic because they've dated this method (or a variety of it) back to Aristotle. This structure is the foundation of nearly every media you've consumed. Even the most creative movies, shows, and books have this at its core.

Why is this important?

Simple. Your readers *expect* this.

You want to delight your audience with the most creative, well-written book they've ever read, right? The next *Twilight, Hunger Games, Fourth Wing*? Well, guess what. They all follow this structure. Even if your goal is to write the next great literary novel, you'll need this.

Humans are wired the same way. We have variation, but our basic structure is identical. Whether your readers know it or not, they are dying to read this plot over... and over... and over again.

And if you don't follow it, things will seem "off" to those readers. They won't know why. They won't be able to articulate what was wrong. They'll flood Goodreads, Storygraph, or Amazon with reviews about poor pacing, bad characters, and things that may not even relate to the real problem.

The problem is failing to follow this structure. The known formula of success. The single plot that has withstood the test of time in the Western world.

It can sometimes be depressing to realize that there's very little wiggle room in fiction. "I want to do something different," you say. Yes, absolutely, so do we all! Which is why I equate this to the *skeleton* of your story. The bones. If this creates the structure of your story, that means the muscle, skin, other features... all of those are yours to choose.

But if those bones don't look human, your end result will be unsettling. Most of your readers won't understand why they disliked it.

But we know why, because we've learned about plot structure.

Great job! You're one step closer to becoming a fantastic author.

THE SNOWFLAKE METHOD

After learning about the Three Act Structure, I started exploring other writing methods—and quickly found Randy Ingermanson. Despite having a PhD in Physics from Berkeley, Randy Ingermanson is known in the publishing industry as the "snowflake guy." That's because his method, the Snowflake Method, has been helping authors since 2005!

You can find it here: [2]

https://www.advancedfictionwriting.com/articles/snowflake-method/

The Snowflake Method gained popularity for its tiered approach to plotting. You start with a single sentence describing your plot. Nice and easy, right?

Well, then you move into a paragraph (five sentences—see where I'm going with this?). But the Snowflake Method keeps going. Next, write a page. Four pages. Character sheets. A spreadsheet. Etc, etc.

Basically, the Snowflake Method is about starting simple and adding complexity until you have a very in-depth plot. Small steps that create big plans.

It's *perfect* for the plotters out there—the ones who truly love spending hours and hours crafting a story before writing it.

That's not me, at all.

I tried, guys. I really did. But plotting intimidates me, and this was as in-depth as *Save the Cat* by the end. I withered into a pile of sadness attempting it.

Clearly, something simpler was needed.

But along the way, those five sentences stuck with me!

NOTE:

I've been told that Randy Ingermanson ties sentences to percentages and word counts in his books. I bought both and read them after writing this book, just to double-check my work—but I can't find any mention of percentages with the Snowflake Method.

But if there *are* percentages in Randy Ingermanson's work, well, that's just one more reason to check out his website! Just because the Snowflake Method didn't work for me doesn't mean it isn't a brilliant approach to plotting.

MY STORY CAN BEAT UP YOUR STORY

My final plotting influence is a craft book called *My Story Can Beat Up Your Story*, by Jeff Schechter. I heard about it at the Colorado Gold writer's conference, and in my opinion, it's *Save the Cat* on steroids.

It's *wild* to me that no one seems to know about this book. It has one of the best plot examinations I've ever seen. This book is what made plot structure truly click in my mind. In it, Jeff Schechter creates a graph that combines plot points, the Three Act Structure, and character development into something that is truly unique.

If you're still struggling to understand plot after this book, *My Story Can Beat Up Your Story* should be your go-to.

So, I read that book, combined it with the Snowflake Method, overlaid the three act structure, added some percentages for my own benefit, and voila.

The 5 Sentence Method.

When you're finished trying out the 5 Sentence Method, please make sure to check out *My Story Can Beat Up Your Story* and the Snowflake Method. They're both fantastic alternatives.

WHEN YOU GET STUCK, ASK YOURSELF THIS.

"Hell yeah, Rebecca. I'm ready to go! Let's plot my book!"

Almost!! Just give me one more section to mention a very important point.

Remember the plotters vs the pantsers? I spent many years as a pantser by nature, discovering the thrills right alongside my MCs (or Main Characters). I got through that time by asking myself one question:

"What happens next?"

That, it turns out, was the **wrong question**. "What happens next" is a plot-based conundrum. It focuses on what I *wanted* to happen next, as the author. I wanted another explosion. I wanted a fight. I wanted a coup. And this desire to get what I wanted wrote me into soooo many plot corners.

The proper question I should have been asking is this:

"What would my *characters* do next?"

There's an age-old debate between plot-based novelists and character-based novelists. Is it better to focus on an engaging, high-action plot, or characters you can't help but love?

I'll let you in on a secret: great novels have both, but they always start with characters.

This is more of a literary mindset. You think back to those Great American Novels and you'll see that most literary books focus on quieter stories. Characters and their emotions, rather than a heart-pounding plotline.

But if we widen it out, you'll realize that we cared about *Twilight* because we wanted to know the mystery. Bella was our vehicle to discover what Edward was—and because she cared, we cared. Katniss was the girl we loved to root for, and because of Katniss, we were glued to the Hunger Games. And far more recently, Violet in *Fourth Wing*, a scrappy girl without a chance who somehow surpasses our wildest expectations.

These characters drive our story forward.

I want you to think about your own friends and their personalities. Real people in your lives. Their likes, dislikes, hobbies. But more than that... think about their reactions to situations. How do they handle trauma? How do they deal with something unpleasant? How do they laugh? How do they love?

Those are *people*, and that's what your readers want to see.

Recognizing when a plot point is something you *want*, rather than something the character would actually *do*, will help you plot a great novel.

So, anytime you get stuck as we move into plot structure, ask yourself:

What would my character do next?

FOUR
THE 5 SENTENCE METHOD

HOLY **SHIT**, **we made it. Let's plot.**

So, now that we're officially on the Plotting Chapter to End All Plotting Chapters, let's answer the vital question: What *is* the five sentence method?

Well, it's five sentences.

(Since you can't see me, I'm cracking myself up.)

For real, though. That's it. Five sentences, each tied to a specific plot point based on the Three Act Structure. Five sentences that, if written properly, will become a roadmap to your entire novel.

So, what are the five sentences? Simple.

1. Inciting Incident
2. Leaving Home
3. Midpoint Reversal
4. Beginning of the End
5. Conclusion

All of those are physical, tangible events in your book. Write a sentence describing what happens in each of those points, and you're on your way to a perfectly plotted novel.

BUILDING ON THE THREE ACT STRUCTURE:

In the last chapter, I showed you this graph:

Act 1

Setup

Act 2

Confrontation

Act 3

Resolution

Three Act Structure

Popularized by Syd Field in:
Screenplay: The Foundations of Screenwriting

I'll be honest. I actually hate the Three Act Structure.

It doesn't work for me, because it's *so* very vague. Certain things are "supposed" to happen in certain acts, which again plays into the psychology of what my readers expect. But that's a bit wibbly for me, and allows for too many pacing problems in the end. For example, *where* does the inciting incident need to happen? Act 1, sure, but how far into it? How do I know when the Beginning of the End kicks off Act 3?

I'm a very analytical person. I love dealing in absolutes. So, let's amend this to accommodate our five sentences.

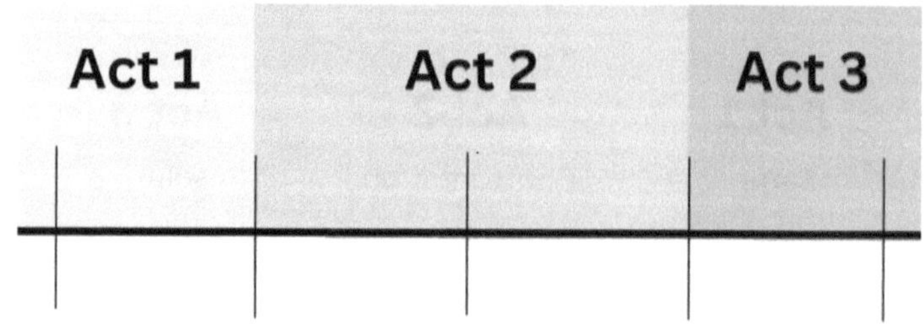

You might notice that I've added a 5th line in the middle of this chart, and moved the beginning and end line *inwards* a bit. There's a reason for this: each of those lines correlate to one of our five sentences... and from there, we can build that graph into everything we'll need.

So, if we tie the five plot points above with the 5 lines on that chart, it'll look like this:

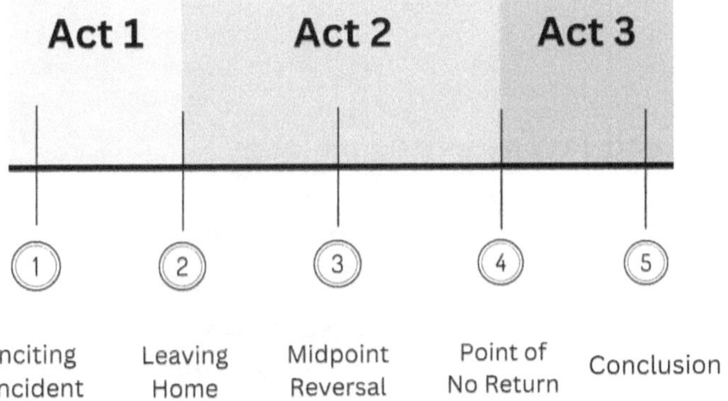

5 Sentence Method

And that's the beginning of our 5 Sentence Method. We're going to tie percentages to this chart in the next chapter, so stick around for an updated graph. But for now, it's safe to break our plots down like this:

- The Inciting Incident happens in early Act 1.
- Leaving Home kicks off Act 2.
- The Midpoint Reversal is the book's center.
- The Beginning of the End starts Act 3.
- And the Conclusion happens right before the book's end.

One paragraph. Five sentences.

Now, let's break these sentences down. Each point needs to accomplish something specific to keep your book on track, so let's dive into what they mean.

SENTENCE 1: THE INCITING INCIDENT

Beginnings have to accomplish a lot. I didn't realize it until reading Jeff Gerke's *First 50 Pages,* but there's a laundry list of things to achieve in the first page, chapter, and act of your book. And if you don't hit them all appropriately, you'll have a hard time engaging your audience.

Again, we don't know if they'll reach that epic end-of-book plot twist, but **every** reader starts on page one. (Unless you're chaotic evil like me, and skip to the back of the book first. LOL.)

Here's a list of what needs to be accomplished in your opening pages. By the end of the first chapter, *all* of these things need to be woven into your book, collected from Jeff Gerke's *First 50 Pages.*[1]

- Introduce the hero and their desires
- Introduce the stakes
- Establish the context of the story
- Reveal genre and worldbuilding
- Establish the tone

- Introduce the villain—or hint at their existence
- Start the MC's inner journey (introducing their "knot," and making it clear it needs to be fixed)
- Get a ticking time bomb... and start ticking it down (something that will destroy the world if not stopped in time. A deadline enhances stakes like nothing else.)

That's a lot.

Adding all of those things can muddle a beginning—and might make it easy to forget something like your Inciting Incident. So, how do we identify your Inciting Incident amidst all that other noise?

Your Inciting Incident is the moment something enters the plot that will change your MC forever.

Discovering that portal to another world inside a wardrobe at your house? Inciting Incident. Showing up for work and realizing they've hired a hot new supervisor? Inciting Incident. Aliens invade your quiet suburban life? Inciting incident.

Before this point, your MC has been living their normal life. After this point, intrigue has been introduced. They're not yet convinced it's time to *pursue* the intrigue, but there's a hint that something is changing for your character, and it may not be good.

But there's something else to note about your book's beginning:

Before the Inciting Incident takes place, you have to establish your main character's "normal."

THE FACT of the matter is, no one will give a shit about your Inciting Incident if it happens on the first page. We haven't had time to bond with your MC yet. We aren't grounded in this world. If aliens invade on page one, we might genuinely think that's *typical*.

Maybe that's a Tuesday for your MC. We don't know.

You have to give us a background before you launch into action. Think about Carl and Ellie in *Up*. Those first eight minutes of adorable, heart-wrenching agony. Because we saw it, we have much-needed context about what happens next. *Up*'s Inciting Incident is Ellie's death. We only care about that because we know how integral she was to Carl's life.

Wall-E does this too. The inciting incident is finding the plant... but we see Wall-E trucking along in his day job, all alone on this trash planet. Through all of those visuals, with no dialogue at all, we realize exactly why that plant is significant.

Think back to your favorite books, movies, or games. How did they establish normal before presenting an inciting incident?

. . .

Now, Let's Add Percentages:

Percentages have its own chapter, up next, but for now I'll give a quick rundown on them. I'm analytical. I prefer hard numbers. There's nothing vague about the 5 Sentence Method, not like the Three Act Structure.

In the 5 Sentence Method, each sentence is tied to a percentage of your novel. This allows me to perfectly track my plot's progression.

**The Inciting Incident, Sentence 1,
happens at the 5% mark.**

That gives a bit of wiggle room to establish your character's "normal" before leaping into the Inciting Incident. It gives you enough time to at least mention the things in the list above before you reach the point where your plot truly kicks off.

SIDE NOTE: MUDDLING THROUGH THE REST OF ACT 1

A lot of people (like, a LOT) are very confused by this part of the story. "If the Inciting Incident happens so early, what are we doing until Act 2 kicks off and the MC leaves home?"

My answer is, "Trying to recapture their normal after something throws it into chaos."

It depends on the plot, obviously. But let's take an example from my book, *This Gilded Abyss*. This novel follows two women—Nix, my MC, and Kessandra, her loathed ex—as they board a doomed submarine to an underwater city.

The Inciting Incident is when Nix and Kessandra spar at the end of the first chapter, and Kessandra requests Nix's presence on the submarine, with the end goal of reaching the underwater city and investigating a murder.

But Nix hates Kessandra and that underwater city. So, she spends the next 20% of the book hunting for every reason *not* to board that submarine. Of course, by the 25% mark, it's obvious Nix can't avoid Kessandra forever, but it takes a bit of persuasion to reach that point.

It's also important to note that there are two plots running parallel: the main plot, and your character's *internal* arc.

Plot and character, right? Both matter. I use the 5 Sentence Method for physical events, but it could just as easily be applied to the internal arc as your character attempts to fix their fatal flaw. I demonstrate this optional step in Chapter 5, where we explore examples.

In *This Gilded Abyss,* Nix is struggling with grief and fiercely protects the friends she has left—absolutely to her own detriment. That's her internal arc.

But there has to be an external plot, too. Nix has to leave her friends behind to board this submarine, and then all she's left with is Kessandra—a woman she loathes, and cannot trust.

You can see how the physical events intimately tie into Nix's internal character arc.

So, ideally, you'll introduce your character's "normal," follow with the Inciting Incident, and then spend a good 20% of your novel having your character fight this change.

Let's turn to Pixar for another example. In *The Incredibles,* the 5% mark is when superheroes become illegal. This prompts Bob's entire family underground (figuratively). The rest of Act 1 is Bob listening to radios and trying to recapture the glory days through various examples.

Then, at the 25% mark, he receives a strange invitation for *real* hero work. A new job, and it pays. This is huge news for Bob, and prompts a secret life of superheroing and luxury away from his family.

See the difference? The shift into the 25% mark should be definitive, something that clearly partitions the novel.

How that looks will depend on your genre, plot, and characters. So, get creative!

SENTENCE 2: LEAVING HOME

That moves us seamlessly into the beginning of Act 2: the Leaving Home moment.

This sentence begins at the 25% mark.

One quarter into your book, your character needs to have a shift into something totally new.

Now, I want to emphasize: **the Leaving Home moment is often metaphorical.**

In the Hero's Journey plot, which is a typical favorite for fantasy and science fiction, we'll usually see a physical Leaving Home moment. They abandon the Shire, they enter the wardrobe, they board the spaceship. It's a clear moment of literally leaving their homes. Their "normal" will never be the same.

In romance (or thrillers, contemporaries, mysteries, etc), this is typically metaphorical. Obviously, if your entire book takes place in one town, they cannot *leave* that town. This is where the wiggle room comes in—you have to analyze your own plot and decide how this event will fit.

If your Leaving Home moment is metaphorical, it's typically a willing shift on your MC's behalf. They begin the new job they originally said they didn't want, or they officially decide they're going to infiltrate the band of popular girls, or they buy a gun to hunt their parent's killer. Whatever this looks like, even metaphorical Leaving Home moments are usually tied to a physical event that pushes your MC in a new direction.

If it's a physical event, you can imagine how this might look. They board a plane to a new location, like in *The Proposal*. They're sucked out of HQ (*Inside Out*). They leave Tatooine to become a Jedi.

Point is, this event can be big or small, but it needs to clearly mark your transition into Act 2.

A QUICK ASIDE ABOUT CHARACTER AGENCY

One of the most common reasons for rejection from a literary agent is that your MC "lacks agency." This is a very confusing thing for newer writers, since it's rarely explained—so let me do that now.

Character agency is your character's decision to engage in their own lives.

A true main character doesn't just stand by and let events happen *to* them. They actively seek out solutions to their problems. There's *intent* behind their actions. Sometimes, these actions cause new problems by default, but that'll prompt the MC to solve *those*, too.

Nemo touching the boat. Wall-E pursuing Eve. Joy trying to save the core memories. Your book is nothing but a series of actions, each taken because of your characters' desire to live their own lives. That's character agency.

It's sometimes *very* hard to realize if your character lacks agency. As writers, we adore our MCs. We think they're perfect, even when they're imperfect as hell. So naturally, anything that happens near the MC feels important and big.

Often times, the Inciting Incident happens *to* your MC, not because of their actions. It's an uncontrollable event that disrupts your MC's "normal". This is fine, and readers won't worry about an Inciting Incident your MC had no hand in creating. However, every moment *after* that needs to be the MC attempting to solve the newfound problem. They need to try and take control of this uncontrollable event.

Remember our central question: "What would my character do next?"

Think about Carl handing off his bags for a retirement home, telling the man he wants one final look around his house... and then releasing the balloons in *Up*.

That's agency.

SENTENCE 3: THE MIDPOINT REVERSAL

This is my favorite, favorite part of a novel. I love writing it and I especially love reading it. Most of the time, I won't DNF a book until I hit the Midpoint Reversal, just to see if the twist is worth it.

This twist should change *everything*. That's why it's called the "reversal."

And in case you didn't guess it off the word "midpoint," let's break down the percentage of this sentence.

The Midpoint Reversal happens at the 50% mark.

So, what is it? Well, up until this point, your MC has existed believing / pursuing one thing... and that thing is about to come into question. Basically, at this point in the novel, everything your character thought they knew changes.

Dramatically, in most instances.

There are a dozen ways this reversal could pan out, depending on your genre and plot. Here are some examples:

- Carl realizes his hero is actually the villain. (*Up*)
- Joy realizes being sad can actually cheer people up sometimes. (*Inside Out*)
- After fighting it for half the movie, Ralph agrees to team up with Vanellope. (*Wreck-It Ralph*)

- Mr. Incredible realizes that he's been working for Syndrome, who is actually an old fan of his, and very evil. (*The Incredibles*)
- Darcy professes his love to Elizabeth, utterly shocking her. (*Pride & Prejudice*)
- The rocket carrying emergency supplies for Mark Watney explodes, prompting his old crew to try something drastic to save him. (*The Martian*)

Again, I use a lot of Pixar or Disney examples because most of us have seen these movies, and they make plot analysis quite simple. But most books have a moment like this, too.

Sometimes, the Midpoint Reversal is a big battle that furthers your MC's conviction. Maybe nothing about their thought process changes. Instead, maybe they identified the evil in the book's beginning, and have been tackling it ever since. In that case, rather than "reversing" what your MC knows, this Midpoint Reversal will serve as fuel to their fire.

However you approach this, if done properly, this moment will leave your reader feeling fresh and excited about the events to come.

A few lesser-known examples. Let's go back to my fantasy thriller, *This Gilded Abyss*. Nix and Kessandra are now trapped together in a luxury submarine. My Midpoint Reversal occurred when a violent disease spreads across the ship, and passengers begin killing each other. Until this point, readers thought they'd be reaching an underwater city, but this Midpoint Reversal proves that there are more immediate problems for Nix and Kessandra.

Examining another one of my books, *Can't Spell Treason Without Tea,* the Midpoint Reversal is a dragon attack on their new town. My MCs are trying to establish a bookshop / tea house. But when the dragons attack, their cozy, mundane life is no longer as safe. Kianthe and Reyna have to act, or their dreams burn with their new shop.

Spend some time on Sentence 3. This is, in my opinion, the moment where you have a chance to elevate your novel from good to *what the fuuuck.*

SENTENCE 4: THE BEGINNING OF THE END

Trucking right along, sentence four is about the "Beginning of the End," which is sometimes called the "Point of No Return." This moment concludes Act 2, and begins Act 3.

**The Beginning of the End is the
75% mark of your novel.**

As implied in the title, this is *it.* All the prep work has been done. Your MC is prepared to launch into the final moments of your book. The plot is almost finished—but there's one final boss battle, and your MC may not be prepared for it.

The Beginning of the End is the downward slide into your conclusion. Upon reaching this event, your MC couldn't stop what happens next if they *wanted* to.

The war has officially begun, and they have to ride into battle or watch their friends die.

After waging corporate war on her sexy new supervisor to reclaim her promotion, the MC is fired for her actions.

The couple realizes the serial killer is inside their house, and it's fight... or die.

There's no stopping this train. They cannot go back to their old "normal"—and in fact, that "normal" is so far gone that they're a completely different person now. All they can do is plow forward and hope for the best resolution.

This sentence is the event that marks that moment.

Remember, after this point, there's a bit of lead-up, then a Big Boss Battle—some culmination of your entire plot wrapped into one dramatic moment—, and then your book is over. So, make sure that Big Boss Battle is large enough to be worth your reader's time. It has to take up about 10 - 15% of your book, which could be thousands of words depending on your novel's length.

Just remember, that Big Boss Battle can't happen without the Beginning of the End event.

That's sentence four.

SENTENCE 5: CONCLUSION

You've made it! Holy crap, your novel is over. In five sentences, you've wrapped up everything and tied it in a nice little bow. Maybe you've left a small cliffhanger for book two. Either way, sentence five is your Conclusion.

**The Conclusion is the
95% mark of your book.**

This seems easy, but there's an important thing to note about endings. Namely, there's a reason this sentence isn't at the 99% mark of your novel. A lot of writers finish the Big Boss Battle and assume everything's good, but your readers haven't drawn a breath in ages.

A good Conclusion is their moment to gasp for air. It's establishing "normal"... but the *new* normal. Your MC has endured a huge journey—and your readers are dying to know what their lives look like now.

Think back to the 2005 *Pride & Prejudice* movie with Kiera Knightley. Sentence five is Darcy and Elizabeth kissing in the field at sunrise. They've made it. Their love persevered. But there's an entire scene following that conclusion—the one where they're sitting together on the huge balcony of his estate, flames blazing and crickets chirping, discussing their life as newlyweds.

That moment is my favorite in the entire movie, because it's satisfying as hell. We got everything we wanted, and I was content when the credits rolled.

(I've been told that this scene is only in the US version of this movie, but the point still stands even abroad. Whether it ends with the pair at Pemberley, or with Elizabeth speaking to her father about her engagement, there is still a very satisfying conclusion to this stunning story.)

The point is, do not deprive your reader of a satisfying Conclusion.

This is especially difficult for trilogies, or any book with a cliffhanger. You're anxious to end the book on a dramatic scene, to leave your readers hanging, to make them preorder the sequel immediately... but you may have the *opposite* effect if you rush this.

If readers close your book frustrated, rather of intrigued, you've lost them. There's no incentive to pick up your sequel at all.

We'll talk more about trilogies and sequels in two chapters, but for now, just keep this in mind when deciding on your final sentence. Conclusions need to resolve your main plot and internal arc, be satisfying for your reader, and offer everyone time to breathe.

OUR NEW GRAPH

In the next chapter, we're going to explore the percentages of our 5 Sentences further, and tie them to specific word count goals to ensure your pacing is on track. For that purpose, let's simplify what we've just learned!

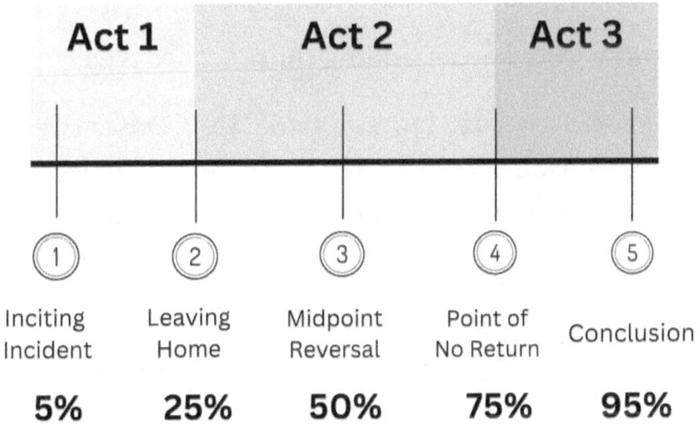

Here's our 5 Sentence Method so far. We've explored plot structure, tied our major plot points together, and are ready to forge into the next realm of plotting!

ADDING EXTRA SCENES TO YOUR 5 SENTENCES

Before we close out this chapter, I wanted to take a moment and address added scenes.

This section is optional.

But even as a true pantser, I'd have a few scenes in mind before I started writing. These scenes were, basically, moments I *knew* I wanted to fit somewhere... but I wasn't sure where or how they'd insert into the final narrative.

With these 5 Sentences, adding those scenes is easy.

Let's explore my cozy fantasy, *Can't Spell Treason Without Tea*. Spoilers ahead, but they're pretty vague—and it's cozy, so it'll have a happy ending no matter what.

The plot of *Can't Spell Treason Without Tea* is that two women, both with intense fantasy jobs, flee their responsibilities to open a bookshop that serves tea. But, of course, the world isn't so clean-cut, and their old responsibilities come knocking.

The book's central theme is: *is it possible to live the life you dream about?*

For that book, my 5 Sentences were as follows:

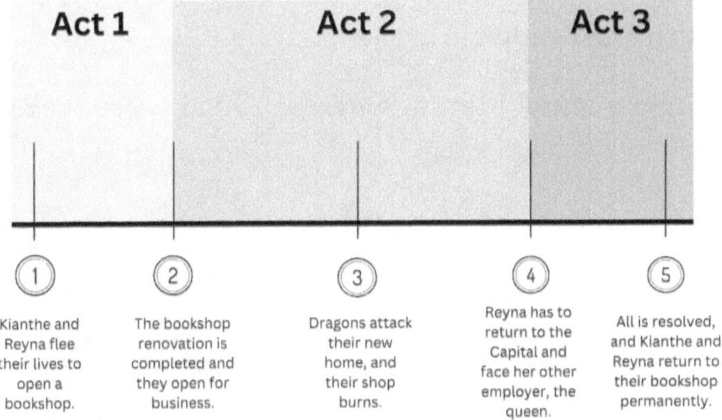

For inclusivity, I'll write those sentences here as well:

1. Kianthe and Reyna flee their lives to open a bookshop.
2. The bookshop renovation is completed and they open for business.
3. Dragons attack their new home and their shop burns.
4. Reyna has to return to the Capital and face her old employer, the queen.
5. All is resolved, and Kianthe and Reyna return to their bookshop permanently.

However, I knew I had a few extra scenes to add—ones that weren't included in the original 5 Sentences. For example, I **wanted** a moment where they drink at a tavern with **new friends.** I wanted some hurt/comfort scenes, **where they trade** off taking care of each other. I wanted to show **the renovatio**n in earnest.

During my initial plotting phase, I added those scenes as such:

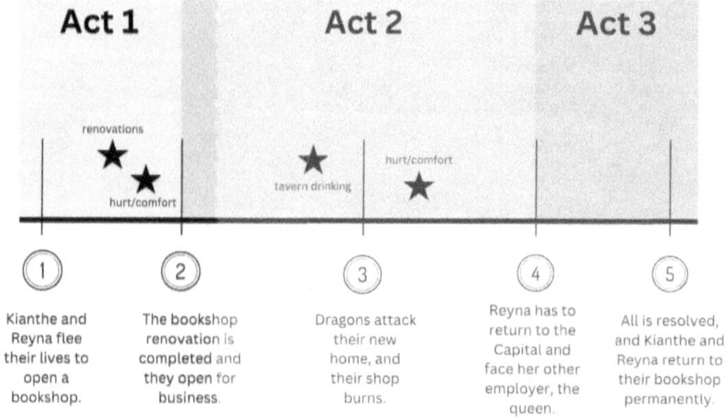

Again, for accessibility, this chart added a few extra **scenes. In Act 1,** two scenes were added (between **sentences 1 and 2):** renovations, and hurt/comfort. A third **extra scene, "taver**n drinking," was added before Sentence **3. And a final "hurt/comfort"** scene was included right after Sentence 3.

Now, some of those scenes moved as I wrote the novel—I **discovered organic**ally that they fit better elsewhere. But **this visual helped** ensure that I wasn't going to forget any key plot points, while allowing me the freedom to adjust them as needed.

Point is, make this method work for *you*. It starts bare-bones, but you can expand it as much as you need... especially now that you know how plot structure works!

Now, let's elevate these 5 Sentences to a new level.

FIVE
ADDING IN WORD COUNT GOALS

THE 5 SENTENCES ARE NICE, but only felt like half the puzzle to me. As I began experimenting with this method, I realized that my biggest weakness was something more difficult to quantify: **pacing**.

That's what we're going to tackle here. Impeccable pacing, based in the psychology of storytelling.

As I mentioned, readers expect certain plot points at certain times. They aren't expecting the book's conclusion to happen at the end of Act 2—not when there's 30,000 more words of the story to read. If the Big Boss Battle happens at the 60% mark instead of the roughly 85% mark, your reader is going to feel out-of-sorts.

They'll finish the book unsatisfied, and their reviews will say the same thing: "The ending lagged."

That's because your ending happened too soon.

**So, we need to tie word counts to
these five sentences.**

We need to track our pacing based on these massive narrative events.

However, before we do it, we'll have to explore a few things about your book. Namely, your genre's word count expectations... and whether you're an overwriter or an underwriter.

WORD COUNT EXPECTATIONS

One simple way to know a reader from a writer is by listening for one question: "How many pages is your book?"

Authors will never say this, because we don't judge length based on pages. Readers do, because that's what they're exposed to, but authors know that page count varies *drastically* depending on the book's size, its margins, the spacing between paragraphs, font choice, and a number of other factors.

A more reliable gauge for a book's length is its word count: how many words does the novel have?

That length varies depending on genre.

In general, here are the **rough** word count lengths you can expect for several popular genres:

- **Middle Grade:** 40,000 - 60,000 words
- **Young Adult (contemporary):** 60,000 - 90,000 words
- **Young Adult (fantasy / sci-fi):** 75,000 - 115,000 words
- **Commercial / Literary:** 70,000 - 110,000 words
- **Romance:** 50,000 - 100,000 words
- **Mystery:** 80,000 - 110,000 words
- **Historical:** 75,000 - 110,000 words
- **Fantasy / Sci-Fi:** 80,000 - 130,000 words

I mention "rough" word count lengths because these are **suggestions**, nothing more. These numbers will change depending on your sources—this list is literally off the top of my head, based on my own market research over years. Obviously, if you go a little over 110,000 words in a historical fiction, you won't be ostracized.

But if your historical fiction is clocking in at 180,000 words... that's another issue. And frankly, it's the mark of an amateur writer, because it demonstrates that you've either 1) failed to do market research about genre lengths, or 2) failed to edit your book properly.

Are there exceptions to this? Absolutely. *The Lightning Thief* (Percy Jackson) is a middle grade that clocks in at over 87,000 words. Brandon Sanderson's fantasy novels routinely top 200,000 words.

Does this mean *you* can get away with ignoring these word count goals?

Maybe. But probably not.

Let's go back to Chapter 2, where we discuss publishing paths. If you're aiming for traditional publication, you have to impress an agent *and* an editor at a publishing house. Both of these people are industry professionals who know how long these genres should be.

They might make exceptions, but if your book is a 200,000 word chonk, why would they take on that publishing cost? Especially considering there's almost certainly another, equally great book sitting in their inbox that's half the length?

Meanwhile, if your path is self-publishing, *you* are responsible for those publishing costs. Shelf space in a bookstore is coveted—and you don't have the resources to pull favors like those Big 5 publishers do. It might be tough to convince a bookseller to shelve that huge book. Likewise, *you* are paying for print costs. The size of the book determines how much profit you bring in... After all:

Royalties = Purchase Price - Print Cost.

Point is, bigger books often equal smaller profits, no matter your publishing path.

Publishers absolutely will take the risk with an established author, but it's likely better to play it safe at first. In my experience, very few writers need 200,000 words to tell a story. Try to stay within your genre confines, and challenge yourself to tell a great story succinctly!

ARE YOU AN OVERWRITER OR AN UNDERWRITER?

After "How long should your book be?" the next question to examine is, "Are you an underwriter or an overwriter?"

Overwriters are verbose. These authors can wax poetic all day, and they'll still have more to say. It may not even be a result of their sentence structure or word choice—they could have incredibly expansive settings or dive very deeply into their character development. Whatever the reason, these authors usually wind up with a 150,000+ word novel, and have to cut 30k - 50k of it in edits.

Underwriters are the opposite. These authors are lucky to pull 60,000 words in a first draft, but they're great at adding 20k - 40k more in edits. Sometimes, these authors do what's called a "zero draft," which is basically little more than an outline—and their book only becomes a semi-finished novel in the (usually extensive) editing process.

Basically, you either write short, and add in edits: **underwriting**.

Or you wrote long, and cut in edits: **overwriting**.

Get it?

Neither is superior. They're all just a form of writing, like plotting or pantsing. I'm all about finding what works for *you*, so be honest about your analysis of this. Knowing if you write long or short on the first draft can drastically change your approach to plotting.

And once you learn to leverage your strengths, writing gets a lot easier.

One thing I will mention upfront: a lot of newer authors I meet are overwriters—but not with any intention. New authors tend to overwrite because they haven't learned how to write a book properly yet.

Everyone starts somewhere, and **the more novels you write, the more succinct you'll become.** Remember that theme, your central argument? You can't be captain of the debate team without a *lot* of practice debating, first.

So, if you're an overwriter, but read the above descriptions and thought to yourself, "I would love to get a finished draft at 60,000 words. That sounds so much faster," you're in luck. With a bit of practice and intention, you can write tighter first drafts.

Find the fluff—you'll do that in edits anyway—and then don't *write* it in the first place. Before you start a scene, ask yourself, "How is this furthering my plot, character, or setting?" and if the answer is "it isn't," move onto something that will.

Point is, writing a great book is a careful process until you learn the ropes. But that first draft *will* get faster, even if you're an overwriter. It just takes practice!

TIME FOR MATH.

Okay, so we know your genre's word count expectations, and we know if you're an underwriter or overwriter.

Now, it's time to choose your word count goal.

Let's say you're writing an adult fantasy, and you want to stay around 120,000 words for the final draft. But you're also an underwriter, which means you add about 20,000 words in your editing process.

Here's the equation for underwriters:

FIRST DRAFT GOAL + ADDITIONAL WORDS IN EDITS =
FINAL WORD COUNT

So, write 100,000 words for draft one, add 20,000 words in edits, and you've hit your goal of 120k.

$$\textbf{100,000} + 20,000 = 120,000 \text{ words}$$

Which means for your first draft, you're aiming for **100k** words. Make sense?

Another example: you're writing a middle grade, but you're an overwriter. You want the end book to be about 50,000 words when it's finished, and you think you can trim about 30,000 in edits.

The overwriting equations is this:

FIRST DRAFT GOAL - WORDS CUT IN EDITS =
FINAL WORD COUNT

So that example looks like this:

80,000 - 30,000 = 50,000 words

With these equations, you'll wind up with a novel that's an appropriate length based on your own writing habits. The key number we'll need for the 5 Sentence Method is the **FIRST DRAFT GOAL**.

So, figure out your equation, and keep that number in mind.

LET'S APPLY THIS TO OUR 5 SENTENCES!

For this craft book's example, we'll pretend you're like me: an underwriter. You're writing an adult fantasy book that you want to be 100,000 words when it's complete. You suspect you can add 25,000 words in edits—**which means your FIRST DRAFT GOAL is 75,000 words.**

Now, let's tie those word counts to our sentences:

Sentence 1, 5% - Inciting Incident

75,000 x .05 = **3,750 words**

Sentence 2, 25% - Leaving Home

75,000 x .25 = **18,750 words**

Sentence 3, 50% - Midpoint Reversal

75,000 x .5 = **37,500 words**

Sentence 4, 75% - Beginning of the End

75,000 x .75 = **56,250 words**

Sentence 5, 95% - Conclusion

75,000 x .95 = **71,250 words**

That makes our final chart look something like this:

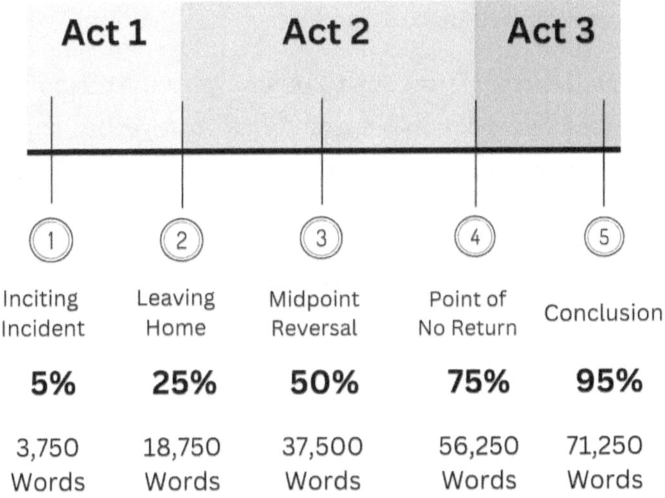

Tying word count goals to our plot points is the final key of the 5 Sentence Method—and **it's how you're going to ensure your pacing is perfect.**

If your Midpoint Reversal should happen at 37,500 words and you reach it at 30,000 words, your beginning is too fast. You aren't spending enough time establishing something: the world, the stakes, the characters, the plot. Examine your book more critically and find some areas to expand, or the first draft will be a lot shorter than intended.

Likewise, if your Beginning of the End happens at 70,000 words, well... you're overwriting, and your book is going to be longer than your goal of 75,000 words. Or, you're going to rush the ending to crunch those numbers down, and readers will complain that it was "anticlimactic," and that the book wrapped up too quickly.

These sentences are meant to be goalposts. Milestones to hit so your plot progresses exactly as your reader expects, no matter the genre. In a perfect world, you'd be right around those word count goals for every single sentence.

Of course, sometimes it doesn't happen that way.

WHEN WORD COUNTS GO AWRY...

I'll give an example straight from my own experiences. Remember the chart from *Can't Spell Treason Without Tea*, where we discussed adding known scenes to your five sentences?

Well, I have a confession. *Treason*'s sentences actually plotted out closer to this:

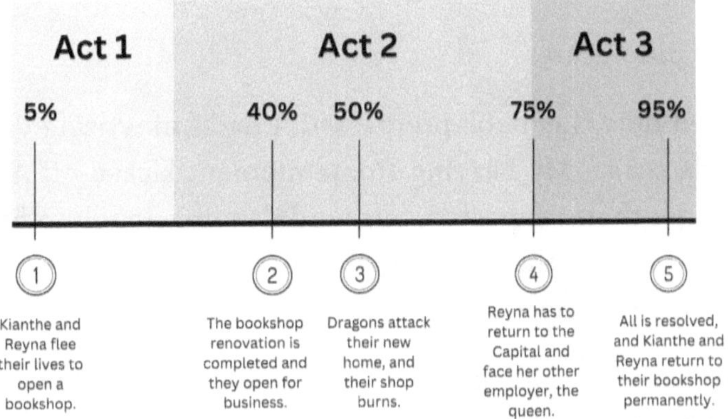

(For accessibility, this is the chart from earlier where I detail the 5 sentences of *Can't Spell Treason Without Tea*—except that sentence 2 is moved from the 25% mark, to the 40% mark.)

I intended to have them finishing the bookshop renovation at the 25% mark, but introducing an entire town, setting up book one in a planned quartet, and building their bookshop took *way* longer than I intended. It shifted all my scenes around, and basically ensured the characters didn't open for business until the 40% mark of that novel.

Because I look logically at my plots, I knew I'd have a very specific complaint: "The beginning is slow."

If you explore my Goodreads for this book, that was indeed a common complaint. And I *knew* that would be an issue before I ever even released this novel.

And you know something else?

I just didn't care.

I liked how this book progressed. I had fun writing every single scene. My Leaving Home moment kicked off Act 2 far later than I expected, but I didn't care enough to fix it. The story had the heart of what I wanted told, so I made the executive decision to *ignore* a known problem.

This is the "breaking the rules" moment we're all waiting for. You're aware of the rules now. Feel free to break them.

And when your readers complain about pacing, you'll know why.

Fix it in the sequel. >.>

SIX

EXAMPLE TIME!

IN THIS CHAPTER, we're going to make sure you really understand how the 5 Sentence Method works—and we're going to use examples from both Pixar movies and a few popular books!

At the end of this chapter, we'll discuss trilogies, which mirror the Three Act Structure over the course of the series.

Stay with me—this is where it all clicks into place.

WHY ARE YOU SHOWING US SO MANY MOVIES?

Believe it or not, movies are a better example of plot structure than most books. There's a reason the craft book *Save the Cat* focused on screenplays, and it wasn't adapted to novels (*Save the Cat Writes a Novel*) until years later.

Movies have to do everything a good novel does... but they only have 90 minutes to get their point across. At roughly 200 words / page, a 90 page screenplay will only be about 18,000 words.

Which means screenwriters are doing everything you're doing, but faster. It also means great movies are a masterclass in great writing—and bonus, they're usually easier to consume in an afternoon of plot analysis.

(Yes, this is how I spend my weekends. Thanks for asking.)

Pixar and Disney movies are my examples of choice simply because almost everyone has seen them. When I break down these movies, people *get* it—and it makes watching them with kids or friends a lot more enjoyable.

Get good enough at plot analysis, and you'll be able to predict plot twists before they even occur... which makes you super fun at parties. >.>

We'll look at both movies and books in this chapter, but we'll start with movies. **Here, instead of using word counts, I'll tie the pacing percentages to the movie's *minutes* instead.** Let's explore!

(Please note: the movies total minutes do not include the credits.)

INSIDE OUT

Pixar's *Inside Out* explores how Riley's cross-country move prompts her core memories to corrupt, which sends her emotions—sentient beings inside her brain's "HQ"—into a spiral they may not recover from.

Joy is our main character, and her fatal flaw is believing she's the *main* emotion—the only thing balancing Riley. Her internal character arc is coming to terms with the fact that her polar opposite, Sadness, is equally essential to Riley's wellbeing.

The main plot, therefore, focuses on Joy's attempt to return the core memories to HQ.

The *internal* plot explores Joy's desire to be needed, and how she erroneously feels that happiness should be someone's default.

(As I said earlier, the internal character arc is voluntary to the 5 Sentence Method. However, for some books—especially when you're first learning to write—it can be a great tool to plan engaging characters. For these examples, I'll show both on some, and just the main plot's 5 sentences on others.)

Joy's external and internal plots run side by side, and feed into each other. Let's explore the sentences for this movie!

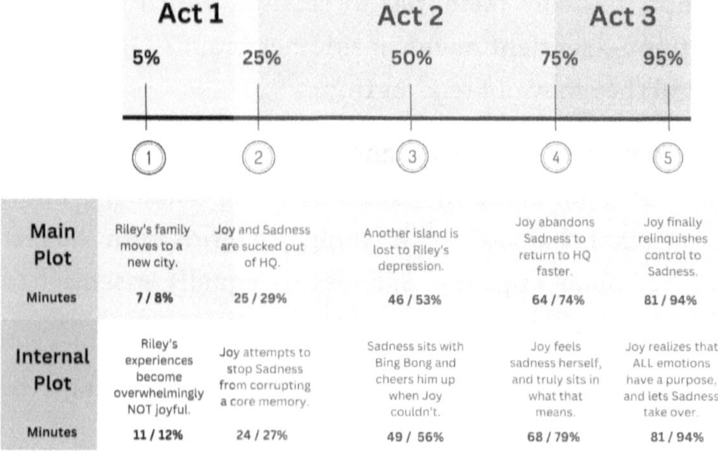

For anyone who can't read the image, here's the breakdown. The graph shows two plots running parallel to each other—the main plot, and the internal plot, alongside the minute each event occurs, and the percentage through the movie.

Main Plot:

1. **Riley's family** moves to a new city. (7 minutes, 8%)
2. **Joy and Sadness** are sucked out of HQ. (25 minutes, 29%)
3. **Another island** is lost to Riley's depression. (46 minutes, 53%)

4. Joy abandons Sadness to return to HQ faster. (64 minutes, 74%)
5. Joy finally relinquishes control to Sadness. (81 minutes, 94%)

And the Internal Plot:

1. Riley's experiences become overwhelmingly NOT joyful. (11 minutes, 12%)
2. Joy attempts to stop Sadness from corrupting a core memory. (24 minutes, 27%)
3. Sadness sits with Bing Bong and cheers him up when Joy couldn't. (49 minutes, 56%)
4. Joy feels sadness herself, and truly sits in what that means. (68 minutes, 79%)
5. Joy realizes that ALL emotions have a purpose, and lets Sadness take over. (81 minutes, 94%)

Got it? Cool. Let's dive in. >.>

Joy's Villain:

A thing to note immediately: **Sadness is absolutely Joy's villain in this movie.**

Remember in Chapter 2, our talk on villains? The great ones mirror your MC. In another world, they could *be* your MC. Sadness is a perfect example of this—the opposite side of the coin to Joy. Everything about her makes Joy rebel as a character. Just by existing, Sadness prompts Joy into action.

That's a spectacular villain. Sadness isn't evil. She's just different by Joy's definition, and that puts them at odds the entire movie. Considering the movie's theme ("it's okay and healthy to feel ALL emotions, not just happiness"), this is an absolutely brilliant choice.

Inside Out's Plot:

As we progress, pay special attention to the internal plot arc for this movie. *Inside Out* deals with managing our emotions, which means for this specific movie, **the internal plot arguably matters more.** You'll notice that the external plot mostly takes a background to the self-discovery Joy experiences.

Inside Out also features a very odd world—one where emotions live inside your brain and control everything about you. Considering that this type of situation has to be introduced to be understood, it makes sense that the main plot's Inciting Incident wouldn't happen until the 8% mark. This world is complex, and the writers needed to give appropriate time to bring the audience along without confusing them.

Sentence 2 happens exactly when it should. Joy intervenes with Sadness to "save" Riley, and the result of that decision sucks them both out of HQ—thus kicking off the Leaving Home moment and Act 2. Pristine.

But things deviate for the Midpoint Reversal.

The technical midpoint is Riley failing her hockey game, because this was the last moment to shine. In Minnesota, hockey was arguably Riley's greatest strength—the thing that brought her the most joy. In San Francisco, she fails miserably and embarrassingly, and loses an island as a result. That acts to speed up tension for the plot: if they don't hurry, Riley won't have any islands left.

But I'd argue that isn't the true Midpoint Reversal. To understand why, we have to consider the characters—and the pacing of a movie that carefully ties an internal journey to an external plot.

Joy and Riley are constantly battling for the title of "main character." And it's complicated because Joy IS Riley, so most of their plot points align. But as writers, we know the true main character is Joy. It's her story we're following—and her internal growth directly impacts Riley's success.

Joy thinks happiness should be the default emotion. *She* should be in control, because who doesn't want to be happy all the time?

Sadness, meanwhile, <u>literally</u> lurks in the background. She's quiet. She doesn't take up much space. In a world of joy, she never feels needed.

The true Midpoint Reversal happens when Joy realizes you can find happiness *through* sadness. When Joy fails to cheer up Bing Bong at the 56% mark, it directly challenged everything Joy thought she knew. And then Sadness steps in and lets Bing Bong cry—which would be the worst thing *ever* for Joy.

And to her shock, Bing Bong sits in sadness... and then he picks himself up and is okay again.

This moment changes everything for Joy. She'll still spend another 25% of the movie clinging to her old version of "normal," but this moment loosens her knot. Joy's greatest fear is the erroneous idea that allowing *any* sadness means Riley will "never be happy." (This exact line is mentioned throughout the movie, because Joy has convinced the other emotions it's true.)

Bing Bong demonstrates plainly that Sadness has a purpose—and that sometimes happiness can only come from sitting in grief for a bit.

THE FINAL ATTEMPT TO **Reclaim the Old "Normal"**

Joy abandons Sadness in one final attempt to succeed at the 74% mark—but I do want to take a moment and pause here. At the 69% mark, the *other* emotions decide Riley is going to run away from home and return to Minnesota. **This is Riley's Beginning of the End.** The other emotions even say, "There's no going back now."

(It's almost like these screenwriters studied plot structure before writing. I always feel that moments like this are easter eggs for other writers.)

Depending on how your sentences align, that moment *could* take up your 4th sentence. But as we said before, Riley and Joy aren't the same anymore. Their paths diverged the moment Joy was sucked out of HQ. In this moment, Joy is so disconnected from Riley, from HQ, that Riley makes a decision *without* her.

That's why Joy's plot point aligns perfectly at the 74% mark. Joy is our true MC. For her, the Beginning of the End is abandoning Sadness. One final, last-ditch attempt to cling to Joy's old reality, her old "normal." The normal where she's in control, the most important emotion. Where only *she* can save Riley.

When she fails anyway, Joy hits her literal lowest low— and at the bottom of that pit, she starts to cry. Because of her selfish choices, Bing Bong is forced to sacrifice himself. Joy caused this, and that grief, that *loss*, helps her understand what sadness is—and what Riley is truly experiencing with this cross-country move.

The loss of their childhood. Recognizing things will never, ever be the same. It's immensely sad.

Bing Bong is a plot device, nothing more—but damn, I still cried alongside Joy as she came to that realization.

. . .

The Movie's Conclusion

By the movie's end, Joy and Sadness are back in HQ—and Joy has a mirror moment to the 27% mark. **She can choose to keep the core memories for herself, or... she can let Sadness touch them.**

It might corrupt them, but it also might save them.

And after Joy's experiences outside of HQ, her old normal is gone forever. She knows a bit more about herself, the other emotions, and Riley's wellbeing. Joy stands aside and Sadness takes over.

Growth.

Gives you goosebumps, doesn't it?

UP

Pixar's *Up* is our first example of a gorgeous plot structure. In case you've somehow gone a decade without watching this movie, let's review the basic plot: both main and internal.

The main plot: A grieving man decides to pursue the adventure he never managed with his wife.

The internal plot: After losing his wife, Carl has to give himself permission to move on with life.

Notice the "give himself permission" moment of the internal arc. Carl's fatal flaw is that he feels guilty moving on. Ellie, the love of his life, died, and he's honestly not sure *how* to exist without her. So, he clings to the past and doesn't let anyone in—he has no family, no friends. He lives through memories, which is no life at all.

And that's his own doing.

It isn't until Russel shows up that Carl begins to see another way to live after Ellie's death.

Make no mistake: **Russel** is Carl's villain. Every goal Russel has misaligns with everything Carl believes. Carl makes the decision to pursue his and Ellie's adventure, but Russel is messing it up every step of the way. Through his actions and personality, Russel literally forces Carl to handle his grief.

We get a proper villain, Charles Muntz, in the Midpoint Reversal... but Russel is still Carl's internal villain. The main plot diverges and we have to stop the external villain, but Russel is still there poking at Carl the entire time.

Let's break down this plot:

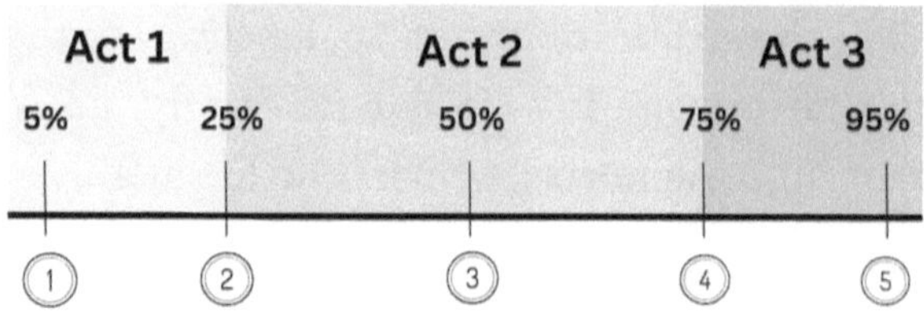

	Act 1	Act 2	Act 3		
	5%	25%	50%	75%	95%
	①	②	③	④	⑤
Main Plot	Ellie dies, leaving Carl a widower.	Carl releases the balloons and embarks on an adventure.	Russel reveals the bird's existance, turning Carl's hero into a villain.	Russel abandons Carl to save the bird.	Carl saves Russel and the bird, and they return home.
Minutes	11 / 12%	21 / 24%	58 / 65%	64 / 73%	81 / 92%
Internal Plot	Russel is introduced.	Carl realizes Russel tagged along on his private aventure.	Carl realizes that Russel's home life isn't as idyllic as Carl expected.	To pursue Russel, Carl releases Ellie's physical possessions.	Carl lives a filling life as a parental figure after Ellie.
Minutes	15 / 17%	24 / 27%	47 / 53%	68 / 77%	83 / 93%

Main Plot:

1. Ellie dies, leaving Carl a widower. (11 minutes, 12%)
2. Carl releases the balloons and embarks on an adventure. (21 minutes, 24%)
3. Russel reveals the bird's existence, turning Carl's hero into a villain. (58 minutes, 65%)
4. Russel abandons Carl to save the bird. (64 minutes, 73%)
5. Carl saves Russel and the bird, and they return home. (81 minutes, 92%)

And the Internal Plot:

1. Russel is introduced. (15 minutes, 17%)
2. Carl realizes Russel tagged along on his private adventure. (24 minutes, 27%)
3. Carl realizes that Russel's home life isn't as idyllic as Carl expected. (47 minutes, 53%)
4. To pursue Russel, Carl releases Ellie's physical possessions. (68 minutes, 77%)
5. Carl lives a filling life as a parental figure after Ellie. (83 minutes, 93%)

You might have noticed with this plot, the percentages are a bit skewed. The Inciting Incident is actually the 12% mark, not the 5% mark. I think *Up* is a great example of how, sometimes, an author should rework their sentences to fit their narrative.

(In case you're curious, Carl and Ellie meet as children four minutes in, or 4.5% into the movie. I still don't think this was the Inciting Incident, but we *could* restructure it to fit the 5 Sentence Method by replacing "Ellie dies" with "Carl and Ellie meet.")

In my opinion, Ellie's death kicks off Carl's second life—and it's very sad without her. But to truly understand that, we had to see how fulfilling his life was *with* her. The screenwriters spent 11 precious minutes showing Ellie's impact on Carl because that information is *vital* to understand Carl's motivation throughout the movie.

They also showed, in those 11 minutes, how Carl's fulfilling life lacked one key component: children. Which obviously comes back in a much bigger way with Russel later on.

Those 11 minutes add much-needed context for the rest of the story. Your sentences are *yours*, and you know your plot best. You have all the freedom to restructure this as needed. Sometimes, the moment you swore was the Inciting Incident is actually just a character introduction, and the true Inciting Incident happens a bit later on.

Basically, don't skimp on your beginning. If you need longer, *take* it.

THE MIDPOINT REVERSAL

Up is another great example of how sometimes, the midpoint reversal isn't a physical moment. Sometimes, it's a shift inside the character's inner workings—a moment that challenges all their beliefs.

Until the 53% mark, Carl thought Russel was an annoyance. An irritation. He never had his own children, and wants nothing to do with one now. But sitting on that plateau in the rain, watching Russel attempt to construct a tent—and failing miserably—Carl realizes his preconceived notions were wrong.

Russel does not, in fact, have somewhere better to be, or someone else to bother. Russel doesn't have *anyone*. Neither of his parents are present, and he's left to figure out life alone.

A perfect mirror of Carl, isn't he?

This is the moment that Carl begins to feel empathy for Russel. He assumes the role of a father figure after this point—a begrudging one, sure, but Russel doesn't annoy him as much anymore. In fact, some of the things Russel says are funny. Carl begins to find himself enjoying the kid's company.

That conversation in the rain is the perfect Midpoint Reversal for Carl's internal plot, and it allowed the external midpoint—the moment where Carl realizes his hero is actually the villain—to happen a bit later in the movie.

Basically, you can play on these percentages. Both of these plots should progress in tandem, trading off with each other, so feel free to align the sentences or prioritize one plot as needed.

The rest of *Up* proceeds as expected, so let's move onto a new plot example!

WRECK-IT RALPH

I'll deviate from Pixar for a moment to explore another one of my favorite plot examples: *Wreck-It Ralph*. This 2012 movie was released by Disney, but I actually thought it was a Pixar movie for a while. It follows proper story structure that perfectly, and has an incredible twist.

In short, *Wreck-It Ralph* is about a villain who wants to be seen as a hero. It follows the arcade character Ralph, who—after a lifetime typecasted as a villain—ventures into a series of other video games to reclaim a "hero" medal, which he's convinced will solve all his problems.

This movie introduces the theme in the very beginning, during a "Bad-Anon" meeting. The villains literally recite, "I'm bad, and that's good. I'll never be good, and that's not bad. There's no one I'd rather be than me."

Issue is, Ralph doesn't believe that yet, and that's his fatal flaw.

But Ralph has to meet another video game misfit, Vanellope, before he can truly comprehend how necessary he is as the villain—and how his entire arcade game rests on his existence.

(Villains make a story, remember? Take them away, and the hero is just twiddling their thumbs. That's exactly what happens to Ralph's hero in his arcade game.)

The plot structure is as follows:

Wreck-It Ralph
93 Minutes

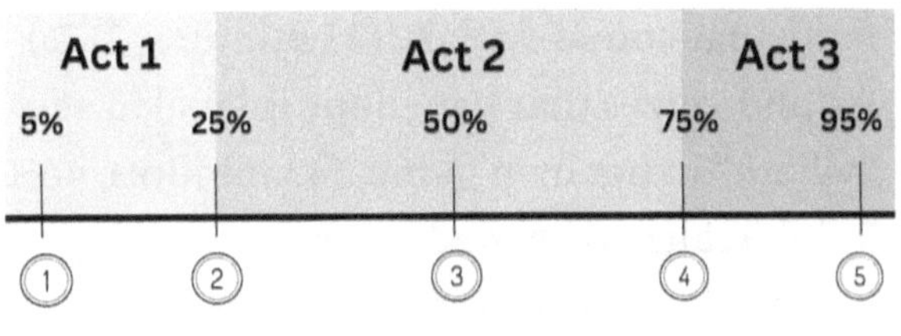

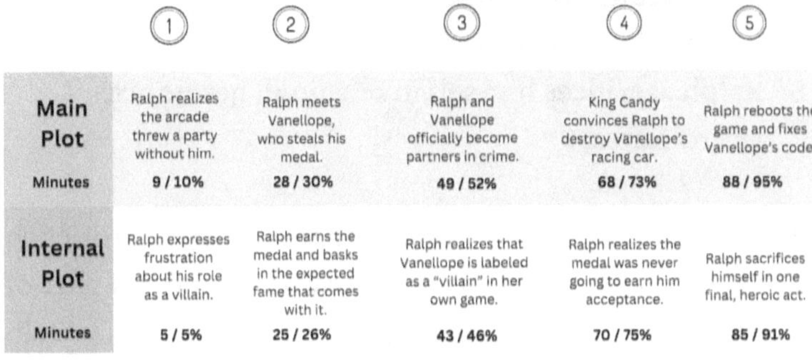

	Act 1		Act 2		Act 3
	5%	25%	50%	75%	95%
	①	②	③	④	⑤
Main Plot	Ralph realizes the arcade threw a party without him.	Ralph meets Vanellope, who steals his medal.	Ralph and Vanellope officially become partners in crime.	King Candy convinces Ralph to destroy Vanellope's racing car.	Ralph reboots the game and fixes Vanellope's code.
Minutes	9 / 10%	28 / 30%	49 / 52%	68 / 73%	88 / 95%
Internal Plot	Ralph expresses frustration about his role as a villain.	Ralph earns the medal and basks in the expected fame that comes with it.	Ralph realizes that Vanellope is labeled as a "villain" in her own game.	Ralph realizes the medal was never going to earn him acceptance.	Ralph sacrifices himself in one final, heroic act.
Minutes	5 / 5%	25 / 26%	43 / 46%	70 / 75%	85 / 91%

Main Plot:

1. Ralph realizes the arcade threw a party without him. (9 minutes, 10%)
2. Ralph meets Vanellope, who steals his medal. (28 minutes, 30%)
3. Ralph and Vanellope officially become partners in crime. (49 minutes, 52%)
4. King Candy convinces Ralph to destroy Vanellope's racing car. (68 minutes, 73%)
5. Ralph reboots the game and fixes Vanellope's code. (88 minutes, 95%)

And the Internal Plot:

1. Ralph expresses frustration about his role as a villain. (5 minutes, 5%)
2. Ralph earns the medal and basks in the expected fame that comes with it. (25 minutes, 26%)
3. Ralph realizes that Vanellope is labeled as a "villain" in her own game. (43 minutes, 46%)
4. Ralph realizes the medal was never going to earn him acceptance. (70 minutes, 75%)
5. Ralph sacrifices himself in one final, heroic act. (85 minutes, 91%)

Ralph's internal journey and external journey mirror each other almost identically, as demonstrated, and it's part of the reason why I think this movie is such a joy to watch. One plot cannot exist without the other. Ralph is his *own* villain, simply because he doubts his self-worth. Vanellope helps him recognize that he is important, necessary, and needed.

This movie is a great example of how villains can shift as the MC's narrative shifts—the only true definition of a villain is "someone with opposing goals to the MC."

- At first, the characters in Ralph's arcade game are his villains. They're keeping him from his goal of being welcomed and appreciated.
- Then, Vanellope is the villain of Ralph's story— she steals his hero's medal and uses it for her own gain.

- Ironically, there are a few times where Fix-It Felix Jr., the "hero" of Ralph's arcade game, directly interferes with Ralph's goals—and thus becomes a villain to him. They have a good working relationship, but there's definite tension between this pair.
- Finally, we meet the real villain in King Candy. And that's something I'll explore when we chat about foreshadowing in Chapter 9.

I love this plot because it's simple on the surface, but really prods you to think about the themes: what makes someone good or bad? How can someone challenge their role in society to become something new? Is it possible to be "bad" and still be loved?

I highly recommend a rewatch of *Wreck-It Ralph*, if you have time. Ralph is a fascinating character with an excellent internal and external story arc.

AND A BAD EXAMPLE: *ONWARD*

Examples wouldn't be complete without a poor one, and I've chosen Pixar's *Onward* for that. In my opinion, this movie marked the beginning of Pixar's death—the moment the movies stopped being extraordinary, and started being... fine.

I was curious to see if I could determine why I felt that way. Why was *Onward* so underwhelming for me?

This movie is set in a curious fantasy world that mixes our modern amenities with a colorful cast of fantasy creatures. It's the basic examination of how technology can seem like magic, yet becomes wholly unimpressive once it incorporates into daily life.

It also attempts to explore grief—but not very well—and a relationship between two brothers—okay, better—and how their mother plays into the family dynamics.

In my opinion, it's doing too many things. Remember how movies are short and sweet? This kind of story may work in a book, but they just didn't have a lot of time to explore all of those arguments here.

Let's break down the plot:

Onward

93 Minutes

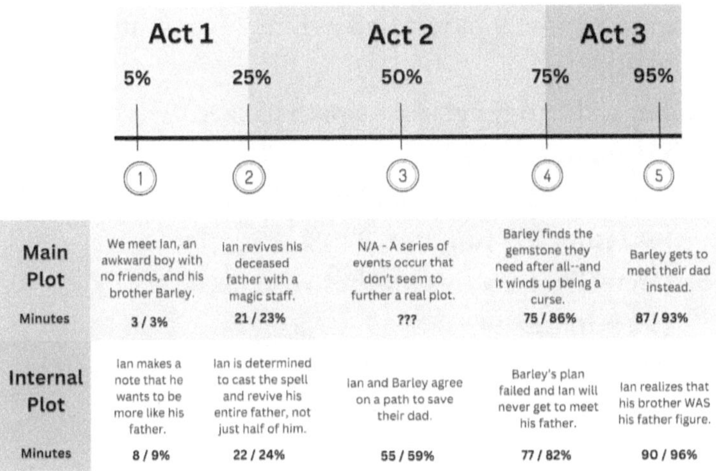

Main Plot:

1. We meet Ian, an awkward boy with no friends, and his brother Barley. (3 minutes, 3%)
2. Ian revives his deceased father with a magic staff. (21 minutes, 23%)
3. N/A - A series of events occur that don't seem to further a real plot. (???)
4. Barley finds the gemstone they need after all—and it winds up being a curse. (75 minutes, 86%)
5. Barley gets to meet their dad instead. (87 minutes, 93%)

Internal Plot:

1. Ian makes a note that he wants to be more like his father. (8 minutes, 9%)
2. Ian is determined to cast the spell and revive his entire father, not just half of him. (22 minutes, 24%)
3. Ian and Barley agree on a path to save their dad. (55 minutes, 59%)
4. Barley's plan failed and Ian will never get to meet his father. (77 minutes, 82%)
5. Ian realizes that his brother WAS his father figure. (90 minutes, 96%)

Chaos.

To be frank, this was one of the hardest sentence structures I've tried. This plot is all over the place, and a Midpoint Reversal doesn't seem to happen at all.

The biggest issue I had with *Onward* is that Ian is clearly supposed to be our leading MC, but he's constantly wrestling with his brother Barley for the spotlight. Although we follow Ian through most of it, there were multiple moments where I wondered why we weren't examining Barley more closely.

LACK OF AGENCY

The other thing I noticed is that Ian lacked character agency through most of the movie. The 25% mark of reviving half of his father with a magical staff sounds like character agency—he cast a spell, hooray! But if you watch closely, you'll notice Ian wasn't *intending* to cast a spell. He was simply reading words aloud, and the spell happened on its own. This moment removes agency from his decision; it'd have been more powerful if he'd sought this spell out himself, instead of happening upon it.

Then, at the very end, there's a dramatic moment where Barley gets to hug his dad—the thing Ian's been craving this entire movie. Ian, meanwhile, watches from behind a set of rocks. But to complete Ian's internal arc of realizing he doesn't *need* his dad to be happy, Ian should have **made the decision** to let Barley meet their father. Rather than watching it happen, Ian could have made the conscious choice to step back and let his brother have a win.

Ugh. So many missed opportunities.

Road Trip Movies

In my opinion, most road trip movies lack clear direction, plot-wise. They usually hit 3 - 5 locations along the trip, and each coincide with a sentence. It sounds nice in theory, but in practice, road trip movies rarely offer any chance to truly bond with a specific location—and understand how it relates to our MCs.

Anyone remember *Raya*? That movie was such a disappointment for similar reasons.

The fact that I couldn't even *find* a midpoint reversal in *Onward* is pretty surprising. If I had to choose, it'd probably be the moment where Ian hears from the other police that Barley is a "screwup," because that's when Ian gets out of his own head and starts considering someone else.

(In retrospect, Ian's a pretty selfish character, if it took him that long to explore his brother's feelings.)

But even that doesn't seem to play into Ian's goal of finding friends. Add in the complex background plot with their mother, and this entire movie just gets messy.

Anyway. *Onward* is a great example of why these sentences are so important to consider before you write a book. **A story can have a lot of impact, but it's important to lay out that impact clearly before you write.** Otherwise, you may find yourself pulled in too many directions, with a plot that feels confusing and clunky to your readers.

BOOK EXAMPLES

You're starting to get the hang of this by now, but let's wrap it up with a few book examples. As before, I'm trying to hit the big ones—the ones most people have read—so we reach the widest audience.

However, I'll challenge you to take this skillset with you and apply it to books you're reading from here on. Can you identify the 5 Sentences in your newest TBR?

That's how you'll really elevate your writing.

In this section, we'll explore *Pride and Prejudice* and *Percy Jackson*. After we examine these, I'll pivot into *The Hunger Games* and make a note on trilogies.

PRIDE AND PREJUDICE

A classic, and an incredible example of a love story, *Pride and Prejudice* is also a long-time favorite of mine. This is a romance in the purest sense, and for that purpose, I'd actually argue my 5 Sentence Method may not be the best indicator of plot progression. The 5 Sentence Method fits best for action-based stories, and romance has its own plot structure to follow.

In fact, if you want a true examination of romance plot beats, you should read *Romancing the Beat,* by Gwen Hayes. All romance stories are shockingly formulaic, and Gwen Hayes breaks it down perfectly.

However, the 5 Sentence Method is versatile, so we can definitely still apply it here. Here's how I'd structure this story breakdown:

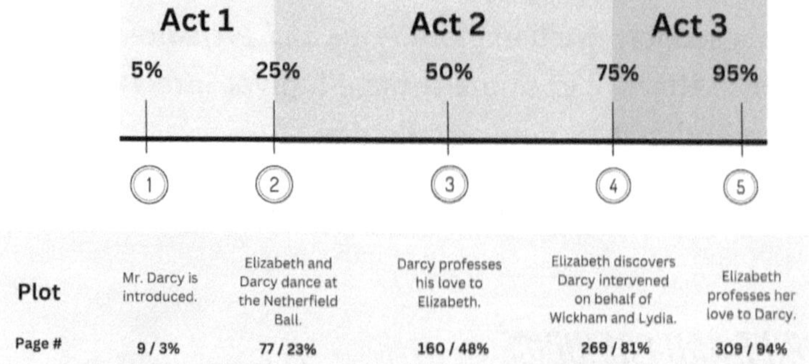

Main Plot:

1. Mr. Darcy is introduced. (Page 9, 3%)
2. Elizabeth and Darcy dance at the Netherfield Ball. (Page 77, 23%)
3. Darcy professes his love to Elizabeth. (Page 160, 48%)
4. Elizabeth discovers Darcy intervened on behalf of Wickham and Lydia. (Page 269, 81%)
5. Elizabeth professes her love to Darcy. (Page 309, 94%)

One thing you'll notice is that I didn't bother with an internal arc for Elizabeth. This is, again, because romance is its *own* plot. In a book like *Pride and Prejudice*, the romance is the entirety of the story. It drives the tension, the stakes, the setting. There is no action plot happening in the background—the action happens when Darcy's hand brushes against Elizabeth's, and readers lean forward in their seat.

Because of this, every major plot beat mirrors Elizabeth's own internal journey. Initially, she thinks Darcy is a snob, a rich elite who's too pompous for his own good. The entire point of the book is breaking down this misconception.

Darcy's internal journey is somewhat similar—he has clear feelings for Elizabeth, but his pride gets in the way. His growth pattern is similar to Elizabeth's, and it happens in a similar timeframe.

The one thing we can see from these sentences is that there are clear events that propel Elizabeth into love. Their first meeting doesn't go well. The dance at Netherfield is the first time she sees a glimmer of someone she might fall for. At the halfway point, he proposes, and Elizabeth realizes she was wrong to think he hated her. Of course, she still isn't convinced he's *right* for her. It isn't until Darcy saves her sister from ruin that she understands how much he loves her, and realizes she's starting to fall, too. All that's left is for Elizabeth to shed her own pride and agree to him.

A beautiful progression of a classic love story. If you want to know more about romance plots, check out *Romancing the Beat*. It's a short craft book with a lot to offer!

PERCY JACKSON AND THE LIGHTNING THIEF

It's hard to think of Percy Jackson as one specific book, rather than an overlapping cast of ever-evolving characters. However, it had to start somewhere, so let's dive into the first novel.

Keep in mind, this book is supposed to be a middle grade novel. At 86,000 words, it's far too long for that, but again, Rick Riordan is the exception, not the rule.

The plot of this book follows Percy Jackson, a boy who discovers he's a demigod, son of the god Poseidon. Percy attends a summer camp for other demigods, and is tasked with the quest of retrieving Zeus's infamous lightning bolt.

Let's break it down:

Percy Jackson

375 Pages

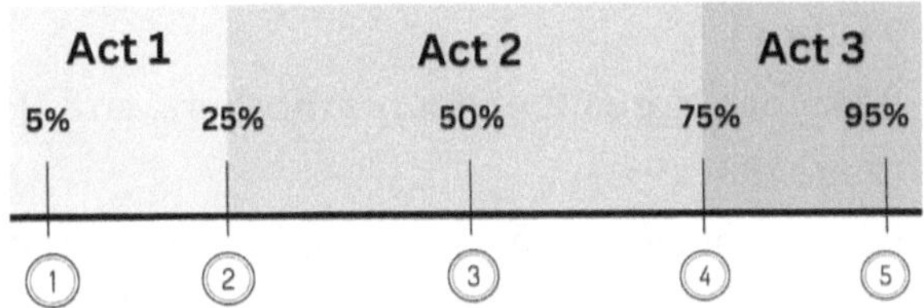

Main Plot	Percy learns about Camp Half-Blood.	Percy is given his first Quest.	Percy calls upon his father for help.	They visit Hades and realize he didn't steal the bolt.	Luke reveals himself a traitor, and they fight.
Page #	25 / 6%	134 / 34%	211 / 54%	313 / 80%	364 / 93%
Internal Plot	Percy thinks his only friend is going somewhere for the summer, leaving him alone.	Percy learns that his father is a god.	Percy has a dream about his mother... and Hades.	Percy chooses to save his friends over his mother.	Percy tries to go home, but things aren't the same.
Page #	25 / 6%	94 / 24%	193 / 49%	316 / 81%	348 / 89%

Main Plot:

1. Percy learns about Camp Half-Blood. (Page 25, 6%)
2. Percy is given his first Quest. (Page 134, 34%)
3. Percy calls upon his father for help. (Page 211, 54%)
4. They visit Hades and realize he didn't steal the bolt. (Page 313, 80%)
5. Luke reveals himself a traitor, and they fight. (Page 354, 93%)

Internal Plot:

1. Percy thinks his only friend is going somewhere for the summer, leaving him alone. (Page 25, 6%)
2. Percy learns that his father is a god. (Page 94, 24%)
3. Percy has a dream about his mother... and Hades. (Page 193, 49%)
4. Percy chooses to save his friends over his mother. (Page 316, 81%)
5. Percy tries to go home, but things aren't the same. (Page 348, 89%)

This book was a bit tricky to explore, and I suspect it's because it's intended for middle graders. **That means it's heavy on the action and witty dialogue, but pretty light on the internal struggles and resolutions.** The main plot is solid, but the internal plot took a bit more digging.

Based on this breakdown, Percy's fatal flaw is a perceived lack of belonging. He spends the entire book trying to prove he's worthy of the things he has: friendship, a place at Camp Half-Blood, a place among the Olympic pantheon. In this way, he's fairly similar to Harry Potter—where failure to achieve his goal puts his new sense of belonging at risk.

Because of that, Percy's internal plot mirrors moments where he almost loses the things he has. First, Grover to a mystery "summer school," then his mother's maybe-death being reinforced. At the 75% mark, the Beginning of the End, Percy makes a choice to save his friends instead of his mother—although the sacrifice is negated, since he quickly manages to return his mother to her normal life.

Thing is, *he* can't return to his normal life. Watching Gabe abuse his mother, standing idly while she lives unhappily. Percy challenges everything he knew at home by the end of this book. And although he returns home after the summer, it's with the reassurance from his new friends that he'll be back.

He's complete at the end of this novel—he has a space he truly belongs, and family and friends who care for him.

As I said, **this is a great example of how genres can alter these sentences.** An action-based middle grade will progress differently with an internal plot than its physical plot events. In this case, we almost didn't need to define the internal plot sentences at all—instead, the core theme of "belonging somewhere" could simply be woven throughout the book with a bit of author intention.

SEVEN

TRILOGIES AND THE 5 SENTENCE METHOD

OKAY, let's talk trilogies.

I want to address trilogies, duologies, and quartets in its own chapter because a lot of authors have their series all planned out. I have chatted with so many debut authors who mention that "once they've sold book one," it kicks off a three-book series.

But there's a very sour reality to publishing—one a lot of publishing professionals don't want to talk about.

That first book may never sell.

This is more specific to traditional publishing, but also applies to indie authors. The fact is, unless you have a proven track record of an engaged audience who *pays*, trilogies and series are a tough sell to publishers.

Authors who do make that sale are very, very lucky.

A lot of the time, a publisher buys one book and gauges how it sells before committing to more. Or they may buy the whole series, but if the first book flops, they'll cancel books two and three. (It's very rare that this happens, but the clause is written into some publishing contracts.)

Publishing is expensive as shit... and it's a *business*. A publisher won't waste money on sequels if the first book didn't make a profit.

This is true in self-publishing as well, but on a more intimate level. If you're an indie author who's soul desire is to publish a trilogy, go for it. No one will stop you.

But keep in mind that it's expensive to self-publish. I paid $2,000 for my first novel, $1400 for my second, and $3200 for my third. Maybe that cost isn't intimidating at first... but how will you feel when Book 1 only earns $432.56? You're running a deficit, and you haven't even started with the sequels.

Because of this, I think it's important to approach publishing logically. Plan for a trilogy, sure, but don't structure your entire first book around it. Your first novel might be all you get for this series. Make it count.

TLDR: MAKE BOOK ONE A SELF-CONTAINED STORY.

You'll hear this all the time in the querying trenches, if you pursue traditional publishing. "This book is a standalone with series potential." That line exactly. It's because of the reasons above—until you're proven, no one knows if you're going to sell.

You *can* break this rule. (You can break every rule, technically.) But if it takes years of your life to write a new book, why waste future years on sequels to a debut that died on submission, or flopped in an indie release?

My advice is to write widely, and vary often. Test out new genres, get used to developing new characters, settings, ideas. You can always go back to your heart-book when it's a bestseller—but until then, you might be glad for the backlist!

SO… HOW DO I MAKE IT SELF-CONTAINED?

Simple. Your main storyline for Book 1 *needs to be resolved*.

Your character's internal arc and main plot should be tied up with a nice little bow. What *can* remain open-ended is a background mystery.

For example, I wrote Book 1 of a trilogy that followed an BN (below-knee) amputee in a military school attempting to earn a set of artificial wings to fight dragons in the skies. At the end of that book, my MC had both come to terms with the loss of her limb (the internal plot), *and* earned the wings anyway (the main plot).

In the Big Boss Battle, she also discovered that there was a dark secret to the dragon war. That secret would have been the plot of Book 2—diving into the mystery of the dragon / human conflict, and determining how to stop it.

Of course, that book never sold. My first agent and I went on submission twice, and prepped for a third, before tabling that novel. Reading it now, the plot was fine, but the worldbuilding was a mess. I'm actually glad I never wasted effort writing its sequels.

Keep your first books standalone... "with series potential."

That's how you'll hedge your bets in the cutthroat world of traditional publishing.

AGAIN, **this is different in the indie spheres.** There, it's common to release several sequels to an only-okay performing novel. If this is your preference and you have the budget, fucking go for it. No one will stop you! That's the beauty of self-publishing.

I simply prefer to take a more logic-based approach on things. If my goal is a paying writing career, I skip around until I find the book that sells... and then I write more of *that*.

I'll be honest—I fantasized about writing a quartet for the Tomes & Tea series—but I didn't actually make that a reality until my readers paid me back for *Can't Spell Treason Without Tea* through their purchases.

A NOTE ON YOUR BACKLIST

You'll notice that I keep saying to write varied, write in a lot of genres, experiment. I want to add a qualifier here for the future-published author. >.>

You don't make money off one book.
You make money off multiple.

Having several books available for purchase is called a **backlist**, and it's essential for any author who wants to pay their bills. Maybe that first book, your soul book, will be a massive bestseller and you'll never have to worry about money again.

Probably not, though.

Even if that *does* happen, you know what happens next? Your publisher will be prepared to pay <u>even more</u> ridiculous money for whatever else you write afterwards. You think six figure deals are great? Imagine seven.

Point is, if your goal is to make it a career, you aren't going to strive to be a one-hit wonder. Get good at writing a lot of books, quickly and well, and your moment of luck turns into a true, well-paying career. It's rare, but it can happen.

BUT.

It's a struggle to sell genres that are too different from each other, in self-publishing *or* traditional publishing.

A good backlist *links together.*

Collecting a dedicated reader base takes time and effort. Amassing readers who will follow you across genres is even trickier. When you're first starting, I always recommend you write within a certain grouping. Make it easy for your readers to follow you from book to book, even if they're different in genre.

Take my backlist, **for example.**

I started publishing with a middle grade book (one barely anyone knows about, and even fewer have read). I quickly realized I didn't want to be known as a middle grade author.

When I pivoted into adult stories, I had to collect all new readers—I literally built a new following from the ground up with my cozy fantasy, *Can't Spell Treason Without Tea.* After that, I pivoted again into a fantasy thriller, *This Gilded Abyss.* Then *again* into my witchy contemporary fantasy, *The Day Death Stopped.*

It's chaotic. On the surface, my backlist seems odd.

But... most of my backlist has lesbian MCs. The one that doesn't (*The Day Death Stopped*) features an asexual MC.

So, my audience?

Easy. I leaned heavily into the LGBTQIA+ community to start, and have found fans of witty banter, fast-paced action, and charming characters along the way. All of my books, regardless of the romance, will have some form of magic involved. All of them are geared towards adults nowadays, too.

Anyone who likes the list above will love my books.

For yourself, imagine a Venne diagram of all your favorite topics. Dragons. Sports. Fantasy. Etc. That intersection? That's what your backlist should include. You can write every genre in the world, but if you can tie it back to your other books, you're golden.

Point is, **don't make things harder for yourself.**

Start thinking about how your career will be shaped by the books you're writing. Don't start in middle grade if your heart lies in adult. Trust me, it's hard to rebuild an audience from scratch.

THE 5 SENTENCE METHOD, AND *THE HUNGER GAMES*

Anyway. Back to trilogies.

I want to use *The Hunger Games* as an example of how the 5 Sentence Method can be altered to accommodate a longer series. Let's explore!

The Hunger Games, as most of us know, follows Katniss as she is thrust into a deadly arena and has to fight for her life. It examines themes of survival, love, loss, and greed, but the central argument is examining a totalitarian government and its impact on the people.

There's a reason this book became so popular. It's a stunning compilation of action, internal struggle, and moral dilemmas, all encompassed in a set of "games" so horrifying that we can barely fathom what we'd do in Katniss's situation.

I think you're starting to get the point of the internal plot vs. the main plot, so I'm going to skip the internal one here. Instead, we'll explore the main plot with its 5 Sentences, and then see how it plays into the series as a whole.

First, our sentences:

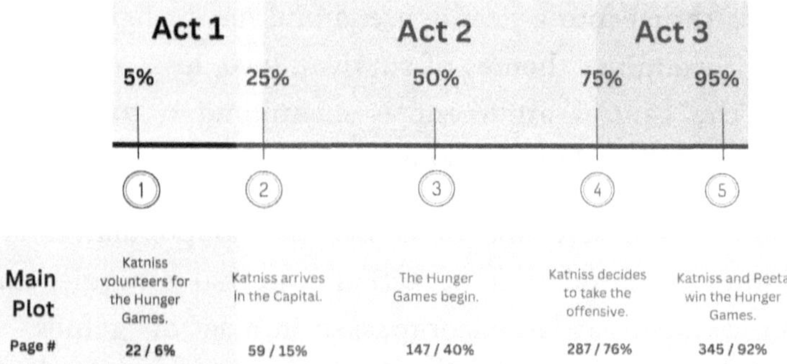

Main Plot:

1. Katniss volunteers for the Hunger Games. (Page 22, 6%)
2. Katniss arrives in the Capital. (Page 59, 15%)
3. The Hunger Games begin. (Page 147, 40%)
4. Katniss decides to take the offensive. (Page 287, 76%)
5. Katniss and Peeta win the Hunger Games. (Page 345, 92%)

Right away, you'll notice that the percentages are skewed. When I first analyzed this book, I was absolutely baffled—until I realized that Suzanne Collins had always intended this book to start a trilogy.

Book 1 (*The Hunger Games*) is, indeed, a self-contained story. Katniss returns home a winner, and the Hunger Games are completed. However, the lingering mystery of how she'll handle the Capital's atrocities lurks in the back of our minds. Surely she can't be content to sit back after that?

Of course not. Hence the odd percentages.

OUR BREAKDOWN

The Inciting Incident happens right on point. Six percent in, Katniss shouts, "I volunteer as tribute."

But then... she boards the train. A few scenes aren't enough to drag out that opening, and she arrives in the Capital at the 15% mark.

That's early. *Very* early for a Leaving Home moment.

This is where the plot skews. I expected Katniss would enter the Hunger Games by the 25% mark—surely *that* would be the Leaving Home moment. Instead of joining the Capital, her Leaving Home would be entering an unknown arena and struggling to survive there through Act 2.

Right?

Not quite. Everything here shifts back. Katniss spends so much time in the Capital—surrounded by their opulence and absurdity—that she doesn't enter the Games until the

40% mark.

Hmm.

Her Midpoint Reversal—the moment where Katniss stops running and starts fighting—happens at the 76% mark, right when Rue dies. Again, we're running 25% behind schedule.

And the Conclusion, which is supposed to offer a bit of breathing room for a true wrap-up, happens at the 92% mark. They win the Hunger Games, then get 8% of the book, a mere 29 pages, to return home and unwind from this ridiculously terrible experience. It's not much. In fact, it almost leaves readers breathless, anticipating a longer conclusion.

Things are resolved... but are they?

Without a word, Suzanne Collins told us that we can expect more. We know Katniss's story isn't over, just based on the plotting of this book.

PLANNING FOR A SERIES

I think *The Hunger Games* is a perfect example of how a trilogy can push everything out of alignment—because in a trilogy, every book roughly correlates to an *act*. That's right. The 5 Sentence Method takes backstage to the Three Act Structure when it comes to planning out a trilogy.

Ideally, it'll look like this:

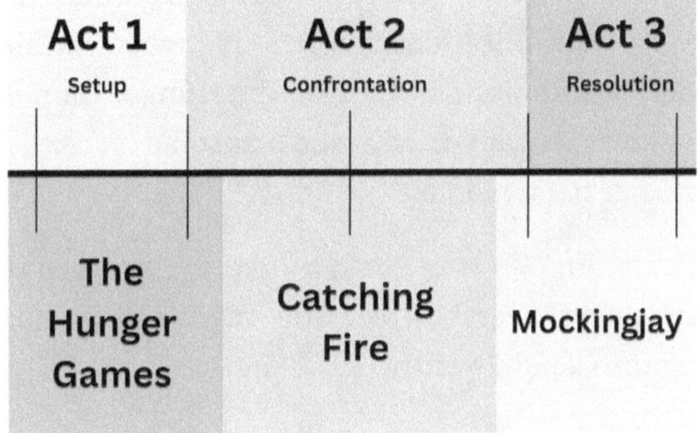

In this example, Act 1 is about as long as *The Hunger Games*, with a bit of extra fluff. Act 2 is its sequel, *Catching Fire*. And Act 3 is the trilogy's final act, *Mockingjay*, again with extra padding.

Remember the purpose of the Three Act Structure: setup, confrontation, resolution. That means that Book 1—*The Hunger Games*—exists to set up the trilogy as a whole. It's meant to explore how terrible the Capital is, to allow context for why they need to be destroyed.

But at the end of Book 1, there isn't discussion of overthrowing. Katniss and Peeta had their act of defiance, but they're largely content to return home and live in solitude. They survived. It's enough.

Book 2—*Catching Fire*—shatters that expectation. Act 2 is all about confrontation, which is why Katniss is immediately summoned *back* into the Hunger Games. She thought she'd escaped, and she's instead yanked right back into her personal hell.

It pisses her off. *Catching Fire* is where she starts to realize they will never, ever be free. The only path to safety is ensuring the Capital burns.

The final book is the final act: Resolution. *Mockingjay* is how Katniss wins. It's the gruesome war that we've expected for two books. It's the Conclusion we desired in Book 1, but didn't get because Katniss was so busy escaping her own, smaller-scale war inside the first Games. Now we get it, and it's big, and loud, and deadly.

THE CAPITAL - AND WHY IT'S NECESSARY

Remember how they reached the Capital at the 15% mark, and didn't enter the Hunger Games until the 40% mark? This is why.

Suzanne Collins *needed* to use Book 1 as a setup for the rest of the series. She had to establish why we hate the Capital, over and over and over again, so the reader is fully on board when Katniss starts burning it to the ground.

By Book 3, we're ready to hand Katniss the torch.

That's a great plot, right there. Never let these sentences get so rigid that you forget how your specific story needs to pan out... especially if you know you'll have the runway for a full series later on!

(THAT THREE ACT Structure works against shorter and longer series too, by the way. A duology cuts it in half. A quartet in fourths. I do think at a certain point that it's not worth following a Three Act structure, but for 2 - 4 book series, it's a good way to explore how to plot your sequels.)

EIGHT

BACK TO THE BEGINNING

THIS IS **a chapter on** writing a fucking awesome beginning.

I **debated on wher**e to put this, but ultimately didn't want to **bog down the** 5 Sentence Method with too much **information about** your opening pages. But we've spent a lot of time exploring plots, so I want to pull this craft book back to you and your writing specifically!

And you can't write a great book without an incredible opening.

In Chapter 4, The 5 Sentence Method, we discussed alllll **the things that need** to happen in a novel's beginning. For **a refresher, here's** the list again, collected from Jeff Gerke's **incredible craft book,** *First 50 Pages*:

- Introduce the hero and their desires
- Introduce the stakes
- Establish the context of the story

- Reveal genre and worldbuilding
- Establish the tone
- Introduce the villain—or hint at their existence
- Start the MC's inner journey (introducing their "knot," and making it clear it needs to be fixed)
- Get a ticking time bomb… and start ticking it down (something that will destroy the world if not stopped in time. A deadline enhances stakes like nothing else.)

Long list. Intimidating list.

But it's important to nail this, because **if your book isn't good upfront, no one will reach the ending**. That's the sad fact—you may only get one page, five pages, or 50 pages before a reader (or agent, or editor) DNFs it.

Make them count.

There's so much to explore about beginnings that several authors have entire books dedicated to them. As I said, Jeff Gerke wrote my favorite: *First 50 Pages*. It revolutionized how I view the opening pages of my books.

But this craft book is designed to let you dive into plotting, writing, and editing to prepare your book for publication. Therefore, I'll touch on a few of the more important points about beginnings… and leave Jeff Gerke to discuss the rest when you're ready for a master class.

STARTING IN THE RIGHT SPOT

What happens on the first page of your book?

Sweet. Love it.

But don't write it down yet... especially if it was the first instinct you had. We all have an idea about how the story will begin, at least based on the Inciting Incident we know is coming at the 5% mark.

But you don't want your beginning to be the *first* idea.

You want it to be the best idea.

So, think harder about the plot you've just developed. Think about the main character and their internal arc. Think about the Inciting Incident, and what your MC is doing as their "normal" before it happens.

Your beginning needs to exemplify everything your MC is before the central conflict arises, and their definition of "normal" shifts.

If your MC is a rough and tumble woman forging a path in the Wild West, don't open with her in a library... unless you're using it as a juxtaposition to her true personality.

If your MC's entire personality hinges on being confident and charismatic, don't insert him into a situation where he's playing second-fiddle to someone else.

Get it?

When I plot a book, I'll brainstorm two or three openings and pick my favorite. And then, just to make sure I chose right, I'll pitch them to my beta reader and see which one piques her interest.

Point is, challenge yourself to look beyond the "character staring in a mirror, monologuing" openings. You can do better. ;)

OPENINGS TO AVOID

We've looked at a lot of movie examples, so I wanted to take a moment and bring up this point: **movies are not books.** As much as our plot parallel screenplays, novelists use a different medium, and we have to remember that.

After all, movies have *visuals*. A screenwriter can fall back on gorgeous art or intriguing character appearances, then suck us in later with a great plot. Words don't grab people as fast as visuals. Novelists have to create that visual *with* words, and we need to do it ASAP.

Therefore, I caution against some movie openings. Specifically, monologues, prologues, and flashbacks.

We have so many examples of these. *Wreck-It Ralph* and *The Emperor's New Groove* open on a monologue. *Finding Nemo, Up,* and *Inside Out* open with flashbacks or a prologue.

Do not do these things. I know some literary agents who will auto-reject if they even see the world "Prologue" on page one.

Seems harsh, right?

Well, there's a reason for it. In books, all of these things—monologues, flashbacks, and prologues—typically rely on *telling*, not showing. It's a fast way to convey information, but it relies heavily on the "trust me, bro" mindset.

Readers trust very little until they know who you are, and whether or not your book is worth their time. **Assume every reader who picks up your book is looking for a reason to put it down.**

Don't give them that reason.

THE IMPORTANCE OF ACTION

Let's explore two different openings, and you tell me which one is more engaging.

 The sky burned.

Stacy stood on the final battlefield covered in blood. She'd just buried a bullet in the soldier's skull—but after the Grand One had entered the scene, her opponents had been reviving as fast as they could be killed. Stacy was losing faith that she could ever win this war, but she couldn't stop. Not when her sister was counting on her. Not after her family burned alongside their home.

Stacy would find the Grand One, and she'd kill him. And if she had a say, he wouldn't get back up.

It's fine. It might grab some people. But Jeff Gerke pointed out a key component that's stuck with me for years: "What does the camera see?" If this opening were a movie, what would physically be happening in those paragraphs? What stage direction would you give this actress?

Stacy stood on a battlefield.

That's it. Everything else is telling, not showing. She doesn't physically move in that opening, so there's literally no action. It'd make for a pretty boring movie... which means, without those visuals, it'll make for an even *more* boring novel.

Instead, consider something like this:

The sky started burning, and Stacy tensed in fear.

She lowered her gun, risking a glance at the soldier she'd just shot. Blood oozed from his temple, and around her, the decaying city had gone silent. But the *sky still burned.*

"Get up," she told the soldier, her voice harsh. "Come on. I know the Grand One is here. *Get up.*"

Nothing happened, but that didn't mean nothing would. Stacy kicked him with her steel-toed boot, narrowing her eyes. The not-corpse stayed down. She squinted at the sky, barely visible between the crumbling concrete high-rises.

The sky had burned *that* night, too. Was Leah watching this from their hideout? Did she even remember what the Grand One had done to their parents that night?

Ahh, yes. Dialogue. A hint of a tragic backstory. A catching first line that introduces our main character immediately. (You'd be *shocked* how many new writers' first pages don't even give me the MC's name or age.) We even get a mention of the supporting cast, and hone into the villain. And best yet, we know who Stacy is as a character—and what we can expect from her moving forward.

Let's look again at our "great beginning" list. I've bolded the things we accomplished in that second example.

- **Introduce the hero and their desires**
- **Introduce the stakes**
- **Establish the context of the story**
- **Reveal genre and worldbuilding**

- **Establish the tone**
- **Introduce the villain—or hint at their existence**
- Start the MC's inner journey (introducing their "knot," and making it clear it needs to be fixed)
- **Get a ticking time bomb...** and start ticking it down (something that will destroy the world if not stopped in time. A deadline enhances stakes like nothing else.)

We know our hero (Stacy) and her desires (to stop the Grand One). We know the stakes (death of her sister, Leah, like their parents were killed). We know this is a world with necromancers, a war, and a decaying city—so society isn't in its greatest shape. She's using a gun in a city much like ours, so the genre is likely dystopian or supernatural. We know the villain (the Grand One) and his power (necromancy). And we hinted at a ticking time bomb (the sky burning), but don't have full context around what that means yet.

The only thing we didn't do is establish Stacy's inner journey, but with all the other things those paragraphs accomplished, I think we can take another page to ease into that.

If this seems complicated, it is. But don't despair. Excellent beginnings are not easy, but this is an area you'll want to focus on when editing.

In the meantime, start analyzing the opening pages of your favorite books, and seeing if they hit everything on that list above. If they don't, ask yourself how that author managed to retain your attention anyway.

The answers may surprise you!

FASTEST WAY TO AN AGENT REJECTION

To sum up this chapter, let's make another list. Here is a non-exhaustive list of why literary agents might reject a book solely off its first pages.

- Poor first line
- Starting with a dream
- Opening with a prologue
- Too much telling, not enough showing
- Shallow characters
- Too many characters
- Stilted dialogue or bad writing
- White Room Syndrome
- Jumping into a new character POV too fast
- Too little conflict
- Lack of stakes / lack of ticking time bomb

We've talked about most of these throughout this book, so let's explore the ones we haven't discussed.

Poor first line - make it snappy, make it engaging, make it poignant. Just keep it *interesting*. And after your first line, move into explaining or expanding the world with the second. Remember, with a first line, readers are still finding our footing. Don't make us wait for stability!

Starting with a dream is the worst, and usually results in an auto-rejection. This is because dreams are either 1) telling instead of showing, or 2) lure us into a world that we don't get to explore. Same thing with prologues. Just don't do it.

Too many characters in your opening pages can be confusing and disorienting for a new reader. It implies the cast of this book will be too large to track, and instantly disengages them. Instead, try to introduce two, maybe three characters in your first chapter, and fill the rest with background cast if needed.

White Room Syndrome is where we leap right into action with your MC and side characters, but don't get any physical description of where they are. Are they in a bedroom? An office? A castle? A ship? What genre are we expecting here? A Navy ship lends to a very different physical atmosphere than a spaceship. Tell us where we are!

New character POV too fast—multiple POVs can be a very useful plot technique, but openings are tricky for these books. Readers usually take about 30 pages to settle into a character and grow attached. By wrenching us out of this bonding moment prematurely, you're ensuring it'll take twice as long for your reader to get excited about that first MC... let alone bond with a second. Take your time with introducing a new POV.

Too little conflict happens in any genre. If an MC is standing in front of a mirror admiring themselves, that's too little conflict. If they're in a fantasy library checking out a death-book, that's a bit better, but could still be considered mundane. Amp it up—maybe the MC's date is waiting for them downstairs, and they're struggling to knot a tie for the first time. Maybe your MC didn't return another book, so the librarian won't give them this one until they bring it back. Conflict!

Lack of stakes plays into conflict. This is what happens if your MC doesn't get what they want. Maybe their date leaves because they had another time commitment, and if your MC and them didn't leave *right now*, time would run out. Maybe your fantasy MC needs that death-book for an upcoming exam, and failing it means they're going to get kicked out of school.

All of these things can amplify your first pages, so make sure your book's opening doesn't fit this list!

And if you're feeling overwhelmed, find out more about this stuff by reading *First 50 Pages* by Jeff Gerke! Highly recommend.

NINE
LET'S EDIT THIS BITCH

Whew. We made it through the plotting section of this craft book. Awesome job!

Now, let's get into everyone's favorite part: editing!

(That was sarcasm.)

Well, sarcasm for most people. I'll be the first to admit, editing actually *is* my favorite part of the writing process. Once I learned this editing method and started approaching my revisions in a logical, directed manner, I noticed my writing improve overall.

Knowing you can edit what you write is the best. It lessens the pressure of writing a "good" first draft. You can make mistakes, because you know that you'll be able to fix it later.

That kind of confidence is one of the greatest gifts you can give your writer self!

Here, we'll explore techniques to improve your editing style.

And again, let me remind you of that caveat. Just like plotting and writing, **not every editing style works for every person.**

This chapter is aimed at people who currently spend a lot of time—often years—editing their novels, but *want* to get faster. It's aimed at writers who anticipate that someday, they'll be on a publishing deadline. They want to edit efficiently, without sacrificing quality.

It starts with understanding how to approach revisions in a logical format.

Remember, if this editing style doesn't work for you, that's okay! But until you find what does work, I always recommend trying everything you can!

A Thank-You to Susan Spann

Remember how nothing is created in a vacuum? I learned this editing structure from an author named Susan Spann, who writes samurai murder mysteries. She lives in Japan now, but she's easily one of the best presenters I've ever seen.

Susan Spann partook in an editing panel at the Colorado Gold conference in 2018, and it radically changed the way I approached editing. The first part of it begins with creating a solid plot structure, which we've already covered. But learning how to streamline my edits with specific categories made everything easier.

If you have the chance to check out Susan Spann's books, I highly recommend!

EDITING IN ORDER

The first thing I do when amassing feedback is to organize it into priorities. I have four editing levels—four passes of my manuscript. For me, each pass is faster than the last. I try to finish my edits in under 2 weeks; any longer means I'm not clear on my editing direction, so I'm dawdling.

(It's the same when I draft. I hit writer's block when something isn't *working*... so I stop, assess my plot, and find out where the plot hole is. For me, writers block is an indicator that I'm about to mess up something—usually something that will take a long time to fix later.)

When I start editing, I organize feedback into four categories, and I always tackle them in order. The categories are:

- **Round 1: Structural Edits**
- **Round 2: Character Edits**
- **Round 3: Scene Edits**
- **Round 4: Sentence Edits / Copyediting**

Why is this important?

Let's say you have a plot hole where the timing of your novel doesn't work. Travel times aren't aligning, and your characters reached a city too slowly—but that impacts the entire plot, because a Big Boss Battle theoretically already happened as a result.

Your options are: your characters miss the battle, or you restructure travel times to ensure they *don't* miss the battle.

That's a big edit. The first option will impact the plot after the battle. This would probably be my choice, since it's often more interesting. Shit hit the fan, and your MCs *missed* it... which creates a bigger, more traumatic problem for them to solve later.

There's also emotional turmoil to knowing they let all these people down, and I love diving into that. But it'll result in you rewriting most of the ending of this book.

The second option of fixing travel times will impact worldbuilding as a whole, and require consistent edits to apply the solution. Maybe they ride griffons instead of horses, which speeds up travel times... but now you have to consider how griffon riders would impact the economy and culture of the folks who have them.

The point is, if you have this gaping plot hole to fix, you *should not* tackle the romance right now.

How these characters fall in love is far less important than making sure the plot's structure is sound. If you did start editing the romance, odds are you'll have to go back and *rewrite* pieces of that romance later anyway.

This is why we organize our edits appropriately. We're wasting time otherwise.

Let's break down what each of these editing passes should entail.

ROUND 1: STRUCTURAL EDITS

We've already spent a lot of time exploring plot structure, but that's what Round 1 is for. Ensuring your plot hits all the beats will lay the foundation, but remember how those are just the bones? Your plot's muscle, skin, and features need to make sense, too.

In my experience, worldbuilding is often where plots go awry. This can happen because the world and its geopolitics weren't considered extensively enough before writing—but that doesn't help the pantsers in the room. A lot of these worldbuilding moments happen during writing for pantsers, which means that you guys will have to spend more time in this stage of the editing process ensuring it all makes sense.

Let's go back to that dragon war book I mentioned before, the one with the amputee MC. I wrote that book in 2017, so I found my notes from a call with my developmental editor at the time. She gave me five pages of comments. Here were the structural concerns.

- Each country was originally based one off Greece, one off China, one off America, etc. (*I'm not shy about the fact that back in 2017, I was* just *starting to write diversely, but doing that well takes practice, too.*) Obviously, a professional editor was able to point out that these fictional countries shouldn't be caricatures of real locations and people— especially ones I have no personal ties to.
- A more authentic representation of my MC's experience as an amputee.

Otherwise, it was general worldbuilding notes:

- It wasn't clear why the dragons were "bad" by human standards.
- Applying the technology to the countries at large. They'd created artificial wings to fly, but still used medieval fantasy-level technology everywhere else. Why?
- Make more of a connection between magic, which was considered "bad" in this world, and technology.

As you can see, those were big edits. At the time, they felt insurmountable, which is why I shelved this novel after it failed a second round of submission with publishers.

My best friend helped me solve these problems in future novels by asking me a single question over and over.

The question is, "Why?"

When you're exploring worldbuilding, explain the world to a friend. Have them challenge everything you say by asking that question above.

The dialogue would likely go like this:

"So, they've created artificial wings that they install in a surgery similar to osseointegration."

"Why do they need wings?"

"Well, because they're at war with the dragons, and need to tackle them in the skies."

"Why can't they shoot them?"

"Because they don't have technology to shoot through the dragon's rock-hard armor."

"Why do they have technology for wings, then?"

"Because… the wings actually fly with magic, not technology, which means they'd have to harness magic against the dragons to take them down otherwise."

Boom.

That line of questioning answered my technology conundrum in a few minutes. Magic is taboo in this world, so they used technology to explain the unexplainable.

Except their technology isn't as advanced as they'd like to think, and it didn't develop the way our technology on Earth did.

They need to accept that humanity is actually harnessing long-forgotten magic. That became a key component of my MC's journey.

This tactic should solve most of your worldbuilding problems. Just invite a friend over for a drink and start chatting.

WHAT ABOUT BIGGER EDITS?

Obviously, that will *not* solve the diversity issues I was presented with—where each country was a caricature of a real country I'm not tied to, and my MC was an amputee. Those structural edits were ultimately the reason I shelved this novel.

I failed to ask myself before writing all these drafts: **why was I the best author for this story?**

My book featured an amputee. I am not an amputee. I did extensive research and have been told I portrayed the emotional impact of *being* an amputee well—but the fact is, I have never lost a limb. All the research in the world won't change that.

Furthermore, this was my first attempt at writing diversity, and I struggled. I used harmful stereotypes in both my characters' culture and physical appearances. If that book had been released in its final iteration, it would not be something I'm proud of today.

There were absolutely ways I could have edited the cultures of those countries. I could have found the indicators of a country like Greece or China—the architecture, the food, the cultural cues—and replaced them. I could have thought more creatively about this world and how it played into each country's decisions as they developed.

But ultimately, a huge portion of my plot hinged on my main character being an amputee. And because of that, I thanked the book for what it taught me... and moved on with my life.

I don't regret the experience I gained writing that novel. I also don't begrudge the publishing professionals who passed on it.

Sometimes, a book just isn't meant to be. If your edits seem that big, turn that question on yourself. Start asking yourself *why*.

ROUND 2: CHARACTER EDITS

If you've made it to this round, your book *is* salvageable, and can be improved with a few changes.

Round 2 is all about bolstering character relationships—which, as we've established, make up the biggest portion of your plot. This can be your internal arc, certainly, but also the external romance, friendships, and other relationships around your MC.

For this round, my editor in 2017 had these notes:

- Boost my MC's personality:
- More sass, more insecurities, a maturity level more aligned with her age of fourteen
- Improve my MC's relationship with her brother
- Expand relationships between the side characters
- Improve the romance—it felt stale in some areas
- Friendship with one of my MC's bffs felt inauthentic at times

Yikes. Long list.

But it doesn't have to be. Let's take a break and discuss the **rule of three.**

THE RULE OF THREE

Good writing plays into psychology, which directly dictates reader expectations. Our brains like matching things and round numbers. We like a predictable rhythm.

We also love things in threes.

You'll see this everywhere. Photography has the "rule of thirds," where an image is divided into thirds for proper subject placement. Interior design's Rule of Three suggests three colors in a room will offer an aesthetically pleasing space. Even in education, presenting material in three different formats can ensure the student retains that knowledge better.

I just used it in the paragraph above: three examples to reinforce the rule of three.

When you're doing edits, use this psychological trick to your advantage.

Let's take my editor's first critique: bolstering my MC's personality by offering "more sass, more insecurities, and a maturity level more aligned with her age."

I'm not going to fix *every single scene* my MC is in. That would take forever.

Instead, I'm going to find **three key moments** where I can reinforce the personality traits above. During Round 2, I'll analyze all my characters and rework three moments where my MC is too mature, replacing them with three moments of immaturity. Then I'll find three moments where I can boost her sass, and three moments where I can imply insecurity.

That's it.

These moments might literally be a sentence, maybe two. Let's take this scene from the novel:

The woman took one look at her tear-stained face and knitted her brows together.

"You weren't allowed to test after all."

"I'm sorry," Kyra choked. "Thank you for letting me try."

The huntress's expression shifted into something like irritation. "Don't think this is your fault. Don't ever think that, okay?" Without hesitation, she gathered Kyra in a hug. The crutches wound up smushed between them with Kyra balancing precariously on one leg. But the woman just whispered, "Sometimes bad things happen for a reason, honey."

Kyra replying, "Thank you for letting me try," is a pretty mature statement for a fourteen-year-old who'd just been told she couldn't achieve her lifelong dream. This might be one instance where I'd replace that dialogue with this:

The woman took one look at her tear-stained face and knitted her brows together. "You weren't allowed to test after all."

"The admiral said I wasn't 'fit for duty.'" Kyra's voice was scathing, and fury flooded her soul. Right now, she hated all of them. "Like *she's* so spry herself."

The huntress barely heard her remark. Instead, irritation crept into her voice. "That's ridiculous."

For a moment, Kyra thought the woman might intervene, might fly up to the admiral and demand she give Kyra equal chance.

But of course, that wasn't how the huntresses worked. The woman folded her glimmering wings and lifted her chin. "Don't let this stop you, dear. You are stronger than the admiral will ever know."

Well. Kyra hated her too, now.

This response conveys a teenage protagonist more than that polite, contained response from before. It also adds that sass my editor wanted. In a single edit, I've drastically changed the tone this interaction and how Kyra comes across to my readers.

You don't have to rewrite everything. Just a few lines can have a big impact!

SENTENCE EDITS VS. SCENE EDITS

I also want to point out the difference between sentence-level examples and scene examples.

· · ·

SENTENCE-LEVEL EDITS, like the example above, are usually small. Lines of dialogue, a brief description, something of the like. Finding and fixing a few of these won't take long.

Scene edits require altering physical acts that reinforce your character's personality traits. These have a much bigger impact on the plot, but take more time—so you have to be picky about where you tackle them.

To fix my editor's request, I'd find the three most *glaring* moments of Kyra's demonstrated maturity... and change them slightly. The above example is fine for a smaller moment of immaturity, but there are scenes later on that can accomplish more.

FOR EXAMPLE:

At one point in this book, a boy throws trash at Kyra—and she draws a deep breath and ignores him. That response is pretty mature, and it misses a great opportunity.

This is a scene I'd change in its entirety.

Instead of Kyra ignoring this boy, maybe she stops and confronts him. Maybe they argue. Maybe they fight. Caving to that violent impulse would be immature, and could lead to a much more engaging scene for my readers.

A fight would also give me the chance to include more moments of sass... and insecurity. Kyra's an amputee who is trying to prove that her disability doesn't define her. A fight would be a pointed way to reinforce that she *does* belong in a military school—and that she *is* capable of defeating a dragon once she earns her wings.

**With scene edits, you should be picky as shit
about which ones you choose to tackle.**

Three edited moments can have a *huge* impact on your story... **but they have to be the right moments**.

Think critically about your feedback. Think about your story. Explore your plot. And when it's time to edit, pick the scenes with the most impact *before* rewriting.

You only need three of them, after all.

ROUND 3: SCENE EDITS

The last section got a bit confusing, because we mentioned scene edits versus sentence level edits. Isn't that what Rounds 3 and 4 are meant to accomplish?

Yes, technically. But remember, each round of edits has a theme. A direction you're actively tackling.

Round 2 is character development. The scenes and sentences you're editing aren't "the whole book." It's "this one chapter where she acts out of character," or "that one line where they professed their love too early." You're editing scenes and sentences, but with a conscious aim towards improving your characters and their relationships.

Now, in Round 3, you're tackling the whole book… just in smaller chunks.

This is where I want you to remember what needs to be accomplished in every single scene. The plot is sound (Round 1) and the characters are enticing (Round 2). Now, we're addressing whether or not your chapters are moving the narrative forward.

SCENES AND CHAPTERS

First, a disclaimer: not every scene is a chapter, and not every chapter is a scene. Let's define these terms.

A scene is a moment of interaction with a natural conclusion—usually defined by the conversation ending, the location changing, or time skipping forward.

A chapter is your natural breaking point as the writer, used to decide how the reader engages with your novel.

It gets confusing, because one chapter can have multiple scenes—and one scene could span multiple chapters.

If you end a chapter with a cliffhanger like, "And *Frank* killed him!" but the next chapter begins with, "Everyone gasped, spinning towards Frank," that's a continuation of *one* scene.

Meanwhile, one chapter could contain a scene where your MC finds the murder weapon, and another scene where he confronts Frank in front of the other suspects.

It's clear as mud, but the good news is, you know this intuitively. Just by consuming novels in the past, you likely have a feel for these beats and can approach edits accordingly.

For Round 3's purposes, I call it "Scene Edits," because every individual scene should have its own arc. However, these edits may require you to examine the chapters that contain them, too.

WHAT MAKES A GOOD SCENE?

This is our purpose of Round 3—ensuring every single scene is solid. A good scene should have a beginning, middle, and end. They should also further *at least* one of the following:

- Plot
- Character development
- Worldbuilding

Ideally, your scenes will further all three.

So, in this round, you're going to want to examine your manuscript scene by scene. Does it move along your external plot? Does it tackle your character's internal arc? Does it flesh out the worldbuilding somehow?

If you can't confirm or deny one or more of those, that scene probably could be cut.

Be *very* critical about this if you're an overwriter. If your goal is to slice 30,000 words of your manuscript in edits, this is the moment to do it. Don't waste your time deleting filler words and hoping it'll equal that 30k you need. Cut scenes. Kill your darlings.

In my opinion, this is why overwriters are typically viewed as new authors—amateurs. They cling to every single scene written, even when it's not necessary. I get it; writing is hard, and cutting a scene often causes you to lose that one glimmering dialogue exchange you love.

Delete it anyway. Save that line you adore and work it in somewhere else.

Fact is, professional authors have learned how to tackle either worldbuilding, character development, or plot progression in <u>every single scene.</u>

If you can't cut these scenes, start exploring ways to *combine* them instead. Maybe you have a moment where your MC discovers the murder weapon, and another scene earlier where he flirts with his love interest. Great. Include a flirtatious moment with the love interest *while* they're hunting for the murder weapon! That's plot + character development, and you've got a much tighter story as a result.

Then, go a step further. Maybe the murder weapon isn't a knife, but an old musical instrument specific to Frank's Irish heritage. Now you have plot + character development + worldbuilding.

We love efficiency here.

BUT… I LOVE ALL MY SCENES. :(

Let's talk about a time when I chose *not* to delete a scene.

Inside my book *The Day Death Stopped*, I had a chapter where Claire, a prominent Las Vegas stage magician, had to ask her employing hotel for time off—which was a big deal considering she's the star of the show. But this book had an omniscient narrator, which meant Claire wasn't present for half of that conversation. Most of it was between her manager, Mr. Hiddles, and the hotel's director of entertainment, Ms. Finch.

I wrestled with cutting that chapter for almost a year. It furthered my worldbuilding, and maybe my characters—except Mr. Hiddles and Ms. Finch are side characters at *best*, and didn't really need more screen time.

The fact was, I could have cut this chapter and summarized it in a sentence: "Claire negotiated for the time off work, much to Ms. Finch's distaste."

Hint:

If you can summarize a scene in one sentence, it's probably not necessary in the first place.

Another hint:

If you can **delete** the scene and *nothing* in your novel changes, it's not necessary.

This is **especially** true for travel chapters, getting characters from Point A to Point B. Unless there's a plot, character, or worldbuilding event inside that travel, use a time skip. Remember, if you're bored writing it, readers will be bored reading it—so save us all the time.

Even knowing all that, I didn't delete it. That chapter was published inside *The Day Death Stopped*, and I regret nothing. I thought it was funny as hell, and that counted for something. It added nothing to the book as a whole, but I still love those characters' exchange.

If you're an overwriter, you have less leeway to keep weird scenes like this. If you're an underwriter, you might be able to get away with it once or twice.

Sometimes, authors have to make an executive decision. Just make them *sparingly*. This is where the term "kill your darlings" comes from.

A SIDE-NOTE ON COZY FANTASY

Cozy fantasy is all the rage right now. I should know; it's my bread and butter.

Things are different in cozy fantasy. Everything I said about scenes can be taken with a grain of salt, because sometimes those filler moments *are* the plot.

Cozy fantasy parallels the Eastern side of storytelling. Remember how I said the Hero's Journey plot—and the Three Act Structure—are big in the West? Eastern cultures explore slower stories with slice of life plot lines. There isn't a point to every single sentence. Stakes don't have to be high. Plots don't even need a conclusion.

They're just telling stories about people in everyday situations.

Cozy fantasy actually lends to this format of storytelling, which is why it's such a big deal in the publishing world. A book like *Legends & Lattes*, where the biggest drama is, "will Viv's shop succeed?" would likely have been turned away at the querying level if Travis Baldree had pursued traditional publishing initially. Agents would have examined every scene for a purpose, but when the purpose is "creating the perfect cinnamon roll," they'd have likely rejected it and moved on.

Now, of course, agents know there's money to be made in cozy fantasy, which is why it's exploded in indie and trad spaces alike.

In general, as long as the vibes are on point in a cozy fantasy, anything quieter goes.

It's okay to have a scene where two characters are sipping tea by a roaring hearth, and nothing else happens.

This is where knowing your genre is crucial. Reading extensively inside your genre makes all the difference.

Some of the things I say here *might not apply* to your book at all. It's up to you to research the comparable titles in your genre and decide for yourself.

ROUND 4: SENTENCE EDITS

Finally, we arrive at the last pass—copyediting. By this point, your plot is solid, your characters are gorgeous, and your scenes all have a purpose. Now, you get to analyze every single sentence.

I say this is the fastest pass because *I* generally write well enough that I'm not nit-picking at this level.

Your mileage may vary.

In general, this is the pass where I control-find alllllll those minor issues I know about. I'll double-check my character's hair color, eye color, skin color. I'll make sure eyepatches don't change eyes. I'll capitalize all the things that need capitalizing, and uncapitalized the things that don't.

The biggest thing here is to make it *consistent*.

You'll likely have a list—mental or physical—of things to fix at this point, so start working on it. All of these changes should be pretty fast, just a word here and there.

This is also the editing round where you delete filler words.

If you type, "He looked down at the ground," I'm going to think, "Well, if he looked *up* at the ground, I'd be very fucking concerned."

(Fun fact: "ground" is outside. "Floors" are inside. That's another one I'll check, because most new authors think they're interchangeable.)

"That" is another one. You don't need to say, "She figured **that** he would love this." You can just write, "She figured he would love this." Or, even better: "*He's going to love this,* she thought."

That's what you're tackling in this round. All these minor sentence edits that will elevate your writing as a whole.

Keep in mind: fluid sentence structure comes from practice.

It will not happen immediately, and it will not happen over editing one book.

I see this *all the time* with new writers. They edit the hell out of one book, often spending months on a single chapter, or years on a single novel. Do not do this, for the love of my sanity.

PRACTICE OVER PERFECTION

Have you heard that story about a ceramics teacher who told two students to make the perfect clay pot? One, she instructed to spend all year perfecting a single pot. The other, she told to throw as many pots as possible, and pick the best one.

The student who practiced more made a better pot, by far. Over the course of hundreds of mistakes, that student learned how to perfect his technique.

Practice is always worth more than perfection.

Your book will never, ever be perfect, no matter how much time you spend editing.

Instead of aiming for perfection, settle for "good enough."

Or my personal favorite, settle for: "I'll do better in the next manuscript."

In the meantime, find authors you adore, and try mimicking their style. Research grammar and copyediting to avoid common mistakes. And above all, write your *ass* off. The more words you explore, the more you edit on a sentence level, the easier this will get!

TEN
HOW TO BETA READ WITHOUT BEING AN ASS

THIS CHAPTER IS all about editing for someone else.

"Oh, come on. I'm still learning to edit for *me*, Rebecca!"

I know. Trust me, I know. But this is important, because some of the best editing experience comes from editing someone *else*'s work.

Editing is a skillset like anything else. I mentioned it before, and I'll say it again: I didn't learn how to edit until I worked with my first professional editor in 2018. Before that point, if something was wrong in my novel, I... *rewrote the entire novel.*

No fucking joke.

Don't be like me. Learn to edit. It's actually incredibly fun, once you get the hang of it.

It all starts with editing practice. You can get this by practicing with your own writing, but I'll encourage you to go a step further by editing *someone else's* novel. And I want to teach you how to do it without breaking their spirit or destroying their soul.

(I've seen it happen before, and it's rarely pretty for either party.)

This will be a shorter chapter, so feel free to skip it if you've already worked with beta readers, or have plenty of people to offer feedback on your novel. For everyone else, read on!

FIRST, let's get some definitions out of the way. In the writing world, you'll hear a few terms to describe editing another's work: beta reading, alpha reading, and critique partners. Literally, every author I've talked to seems to have a different definition of what these are.

For this craft book, let's break them into these categories:

Beta Reader:

- A first-line reader who reads your book after your initial edits, and offers feedback for a second or third round of edits.
- This person can be another author, or just a reader.

Alpha Reader

- A person who receives your first draft in its rawest form, without any edits applied beforehand. Sometimes, these readers are sent chapters the minute the author is finished with them, to offer feedback in real time.
- This person can be another author, a reader, or sometimes a loved one.

Critique Partner

- An exchange of work between two authors, either at the alpha or beta phase. Critique partners are sometimes paired together in a workshop, attend a physical critique group, or meet online.
- This is typically author-to-author.

Another level of feedback can come from ARC readers—or Advanced Reader Copy readers. These folks read your book after edits are done, but before the book is released, and hopefully review your book online. They're typically used in both traditional and indie publishing to gauge public sentiment on a new release.

ARC readers are not meant for editing feedback. By the time your manuscript reaches ARC readers, it's usually too late for sweeping changes. I ask my ARC readers to offer insight on sensitivity issues, vibes, and that's about it.

For the purposes of this chapter, we'll be focusing primarily on beta reading and critique partners.

As I said, many authors—myself included—use these terms interchangeably. There's a lot of overlap, as we'll see below.

We won't worry too much about alpha readers. Why? Well, you likely already know who your alpha readers are —they're the people closest to you, the ones who are dying to read your work just because they love you. They're helpful, but they aren't always the most reliable form of feedback.

As much as I adore my family's feedback, they *have* to like my stuff.

So, I find beta readers instead.

FINISH *AND EDIT* THE BOOK FIRST.

If you've even touched publishing spaces, you'll know that everyone is looking for beta readers. Authors of every genre and experience level need fresh readers to offer feedback on their books.

The beta reader / author relationship can look different for everyone. Some people exchange chapters as they're writing them, so the other person can offer feedback in real time. Some offer line-by-line edits, and some prefer sweeping generalizations of things to fix. This is between you and your beta reader; everyone's preferences are different.

I can understand why you're eager for that kind of feedback. It's exciting stuff!

But please, slow your roll.

Ideally, you should get your manuscript to 85% perfect before handing it off to a beta reader.

You don't want to waste anyone's time with unedited mush. A beta reader's time is precious, and they're doing you a massive favor. You owe it to the person reading your book to get it in the *best* shape possible before sending it over for comments.

Polish the shit out of it, and once you think it's ready for a literary agent's eyes... find beta readers to tell you flatly, "It isn't."

Hopefully they'll be nicer than that, but the point stands.

WHERE TO FIND A BETA READER

Okay, your book is ready.

Now, where do you find these elusive beta readers?

All over. There is no shortage of people who want to read your novel—which I know sounds suspicious to some of you. I promise, it's true, as long as you make your novel as best as it can be, and follow proper etiquette when hunting for beta readers.

First, look at who you already know. I actually found great betas in my **high school and college friends**. Most were avid readers, so even though they didn't know writing convention, they were excellent at pinpointing genre expectations.

You can check **local writing groups**—your library might have some available! There's usually some kind of writing group in every major city, so reach out and attend some of their events. Or Meetup is another option! I've met great betas all over.

The final place to check is **social media**. Discord servers, TikTok, Instagram, Facebook groups, Threads. Anywhere writers and readers gather, you'll find people interested in beta reading.

PROPER ETIQUETTE

Now that you've found a beta reader, let's talk about that etiquette. There are two kinds of beta readers: those who are just readers, and those who are also authors.

There is different etiquette depending on who you're dealing with.

. . .

IF YOUR BETA **reader is just a reader**, always remember that you are asking a stranger for a huge dedication of time and energy. Sometimes you're asking under deadline.

The pleasure of reading your book is not enough.

These readers deserve your praise and heartfelt appreciation. Whatever feedback they give, you take with a smile—whether or not you plan to implement it.

These readers are doing you a service. Oftentimes, for free. Even if they're a paid beta reader, industry rate is so low for a full-length novel that they're making pennies.

I choose 3 - 8 beta readers for my books, and I always get their addresses. Many of them get mentions in my acknowledgements, but at the very least, I'll mail them a physical copy of the book once it's published.

Never take a beta reader for granted. Treat them well, and these readers can become your biggest advocates and longtime fans.

And for the love of everything holy, *never* get online to complain about how they:

1. didn't finish your novel in your desired timeframe.
2. didn't give the kind of feedback you wanted.
3. didn't leave a review.
4. gave you a 4 star review instead of a 5 star.

Don't be that author causing drama on social media because they felt they were owed something. They give the rest of us a bad name.

Now, if your beta reader is also an author, the etiquette is a bit different. I want you to imagine you're a member of a writing server on Discord, where you're all working hard towards finishing your novels. Someone new joins, and immediately posts in the feedback channel that they "need someone to read their book."

When no one responds—because none of you *know* this person—they get miffed. "No one's reading this? It's better than anything you've ever read. You all suck. Why isn't anyone responding????"

Hmm. I wonder.

Friendship between authors goes a long way, and finding good beta readers often requires **equal exchange**. If you're asking for feedback, you'd damn well better be *giving* feedback, or helping them somehow.

As you can imagine, this is where the definitions begin to muddle—technically, this means you've also found a critique partner. My beta reader became my critique partner, and then became my alpha reader. It got complicated.

But it started with an equal exchange of work. We made each other better writers, just by editing each others' things.

HOW TO WORK WITH YOUR NEW BETA

Once you find a beta reader, the question shifts into how you will work together. Here are some tips to secure a positive relationship with your new beta reader!

TIP #1: Only offer to exchange a chapter at first.

This applies to both authors and readers. Never commit to more than a chapter upfront. It's tempting to offer a full manuscript for editing, but this beta reader may be disastrous to work with. They may completely miss the point of your novel. Or they may just have time constraints that keep them from reading.

Regardless of your initial vibes, start small. You can always send more of the manuscript later, but smaller commitments are easier on both sides. Gauge how they offer feedback, gauge how you feel *receiving* their feedback, and make an educated decision about whether to continue with more.

TIP #2: Follow the Compliment Sandwich.

The Compliment Sandwich is an easy way to ensure no one's feelings are hurt while offering feedback. It's tempting to say, "this needs fixing," but that's too blunt and is usually received poorly. I've seen many authors floundering after "scathing" beta reader feedback.

So, have a conversation before you start, and make sure you're both okay using the Compliment Sandwich. It looks like this:

Compliment | Constructive Criticism | Compliment

Start with a compliment. "I really loved the characterization in this chapter." Then move into *constructive* criticism, not flat-out critique. "My one concern was that your MC felt a bit out of character here. She came across as pretty bossy, but I don't think that's her personality…" Then finish with a compliment: "But I still think the chapter as a whole was amazing!"

This format helps keep things positive and encouraging, which is crucial to most authors and their creative process.

TIP #3: Use softer language.

You may notice my tone in that last example. I used words like "one concern," "a bit," "pretty," and "I don't think…" All of those soften my thoughts—that the MC was out of character—without being rude.

One of the biggest and easiest triggers for authors is when a critique partner or beta responds with some comment like, "You need to change this." Or, "You have to fix her character." This kind of concrete language can actually come across as insulting, because it implies that the beta reader knows more about your book than you do.

So, getting on the same page about this kind of feedback can save a relationship before it sours.

Tɪᴘ #4: Whether they take your feedback is not your concern.

Let me reiterate.

IT DOES NOT AFFECT YOU IF THEY TAKE YOUR FEEDBACK OR NOT.

I get it. You spent a lot of time on those edits, and compared to the writer you're critiquing, you're a goddamn expert. Clearly, they haven't researched plot structure as well as you, or built a world as complex. Their sentence structure is abysmal. You obviously know more about writing.

See where I'm going with this?

It's easy to feel arrogant when we're reading something and perceiving our own writing as better. I fall into this trap *all the time*, and I'm constantly reeling myself back into a proper frame of mind. I'm learning. You're learning. That person you're critiquing? They're learning too.

They may not learn as fast, or apply things well enough to avoid making a fool of themselves... but that's a learning process too.

Sometimes, authors *need* to query shit stories just to learn how to stomach rejection.

And another fact: they know their story better than you.

They wrote it, after all. So, when you hand them feedback and are convinced it'll improve all problems, remember that it's *not your concern* if they implement your feedback. You fulfilled your half of the deal by handing comments over. What happens next is their choice, not yours.

Take a breath and focus on your own edits. Odds are, you have some things to fix in your own book, too. ;)

BETA READER TAKEAWAYS

Regardless of how you find them, connecting with a beta reader or critique partner is *amazing*. It takes a while to warm up—most relationships do—but after that it's legendary.

Beta reading is one of the best ways to learn how to edit, simply because you're editing work you're unfamiliar with. You'll learn how to identify plot problems in their work, and that will translate to your own writing. And if you become good enough friends, you might even find a brainstorming partner—someone who can help you plot future novels!

There's nothing better than pouring a glass of wine and connecting with your beta reader over a new world you're excited to share.

Basically, editing is scary. Take a friend!

Now that we've discussed giving and receiving feedback, let's move back into some writing craft tips and tricks! We're almost there, guys.

ELEVEN

WRITING TIPS THAT DIDN'T FIT ANYWHERE ELSE

THIS IS THE WRAP-UP CHAPTER, where we explore tidbits that have helped me immensely over my writing career, but don't fit nicely into little chapters like everything else.

Get prepared for the miscellaneous writing tips chapter!

BLANK SPACE ON A PAGE

This section is aimed at visual readers—or authors who want to entertain visual readers. Anyone who reads in physical book or ebook format will benefit from this!

First, a test. Don't try to read the image below. Just take a look at these two book pages, a fast glance—like you're in a bookstore, skimming for your next purchase.

Which one would you want to buy?

Ten bucks says that you thought, instantly, "The left one."

(For accessibility, the image above features two distant, unreadable images of two book pages. The left page has more dialogue, double spacing, and lots of blank space. The right image is denser, with little spacing, misspelled words, and very little dialogue.)

There's a psychological reason for this, believe it or not.

The right image is dense. It looks like it might not be formatted properly. There's a squiggly red line, implying a potential spelling error—which means it might not be fully edited. In general, your brain probably looked at that image and said, "Ugh, this is going to be a slog. Better get into a learning mindset, instead of an enjoyment one."

The left image, meanwhile, has more spacing between the lines, a steeper indentation, clear dialogue. It just looks more inviting.

It's because of blank space on that left page.

We're fiction writers—which means no one's reading our books to learn something. They're reading to enjoy. To forget. To feel like someone else for a while. It's a pleasurable experience—sometimes literally, depending on spice level—and the last thing they want to see when they open a book is a huge block of text.

Which means that *as* fiction writers,
paragraphs are our friends.
Use them liberally.

A reader makes a snap judgement unconsciously when they open your book. Before they even start reading, their brain is assessing the text as a whole—and deciding if it'll be "hard" or not. The brain will think: *How much energy am I going to expend here?*

Sad thing is, brains are inherently lazy. If the answer is, "Looks tough. Probably a lot of energy," most readers will shrug and put the book down. There are dozens more that took advantage of blank space on the page, after all.

This seems silly, but it was an "ah hah" moment for me as a teenager. Blank space on a page makes a big difference. Please don't write paragraphs that drag—your readers will thank you for it later.

DICTATING READING SPEED

While we're on the topic of psychology and reading, let's chat about sentence structure.

READING SPEED BY CHAPTER:

Have you ever read a book by James Patterson? Most of them have incredibly short chapters—several of his books are actually quite short in word count length, but you wouldn't know because there are a hundred chapters inside one book.

That's by design.

James Patterson leans into the dopamine rush your brain offers when you finish something. His books offer your brain a literal reward at the end of every chapter, because they're so short you can *fly* through them. And that lends to a feeling of accomplishment.

It also traps readers in the book. When your chapters are long, a reader's "just one more page" becomes, "No, shit, I *really* have to get to bed, or I'll be screwed tomorrow." Now, I'm not saying we all hope our readers are sleep deprived because of our books, but I think we can all agree it's a huge compliment when we keep them up overnight. >.>

If you offer clean, easily attainable endings, a reader won't have a problem saying, "Well, the chapters are so short.

Maybe one more." And then you have another chance to hook them with a cliffhanger—and keep that cycle going.

To be clear, I am *not* advocating that you mirror James Patterson's hyper-short chapters. Most readers have a longer attention span than that, and several of my friends get annoyed by how many chapters he uses. However, it's important to pay attention to word count length for your chapters. Every writer has a different sweet spot, but you definitely don't want them topping 7,000 words or more.

My sweet spot is 2,000 - 4,000 words / chapter, personally. My books usually have 27 - 36 chapters, depending on length and genre. But if I really want a reader to keep turning pages, I'll consciously shorten the chapter length just to play off this psychological trick.

READING SPEED BY SENTENCE:

Here's another trick for you. Reading actually causes true emotions in your brain and body. You feel the same thing for your book boyfriend as you do your actual partner—in your brain, it's the same chemical release. When you "fall in love" with a character, you are quite literally falling in love.

Your body can't tell the difference between fiction and reality, and that's something authors can use.

When you're writing an action scene, or something intense, you likely want your reader's heart to be pounding alongside your MC's. You *want* them to have sweaty palms, for them to pull the book closer, because all that matters is whether or not your character survives.

Sentences can be a powerful way to elicit that emotion.

Short sentences are fast. They're easy to read. They let you fly through a paragraph. Stacked on top of each other, they can create a staccato effect that mimics a beating heart. Boom. Boom. Boom.

Meanwhile, longer sentences are more fluid. You can start off slow, ease your reader into it. Then, right as they're feeling comfortable, you create a run-on sentence, something that feels like a character sprinting through a haunted house, feeling the brushing fingers of a ghost at their back, ice slicing down their spine, but the door is there, *right* there, and if they just take another step they might escape—

See what I did there?

Another tactic is mimicking our speaking habits. When we want to imply something is important, we *pause* after saying it. That pause—that moment for your audience to contemplate what was said—lends weight to your words.

Paragraphs are our pauses.

By using paragraphs like I just did above, it's singling out a line for your reader to notice. Their eyes may glaze over this paragraph, but they'll damn well read that phrase, "paragraphs are our pauses."

. . .

THE KEY to all these tactics is moderation. You don't want to overload a reader with strange sentence structure *all the time*. It'll lose its effect. The goal is to use these techniques as seamlessly as possible, so most readers don't even realize you're doing it.

But when their hearts start to pound, or they gasp quietly and cover their mouth, or they're so engrossed that the world around them fades... that's when you know you've done it right.

CHOOSING A POV

I hate multi-POV books.

Think about what another POV accomplishes. It offers an inside look at a new character—often with a very different life from your MC. It lets you *show* their life, their struggles, their world, with ease. A lot of people love this.

Read this:

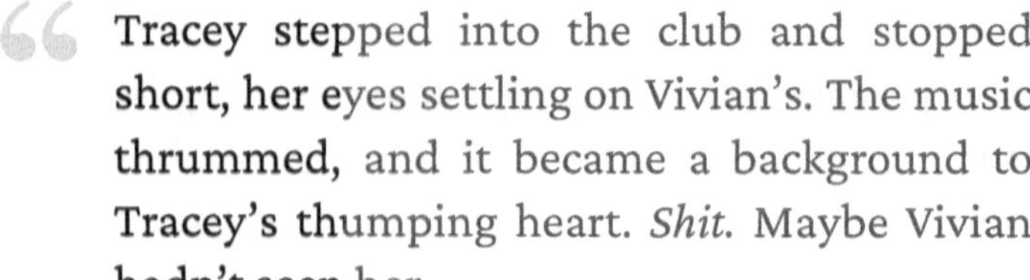

Tracey stepped into the club and stopped short, her eyes settling on Vivian's. The music thrummed, and it became a background to Tracey's thumping heart. *Shit*. Maybe Vivian hadn't seen her.

Carefully, Tracey turned away, angling for the entrance.

"CiCi, is that you?" a sing-song voice called. "What are you doing out here, all alone...? And without your pistol, no less." Vivian's voice dropped an octave. "How unfortunate."

We don't know the history behind Tracey and Vivian, but we know there damn well is one. We know Vivian has a maybe-rude nickname for Tracey. We know this might turn violent.

Do we need to know more? How vital is it to swap in the next chapter to Vivian's point of view, just to show us her life and desires? It's already pretty clear she runs this club. It's obvious that she's dangerous.

Frankly, I'm more interested in how Tracey is going to escape—and how she'll feel after seeing Vivian again.

One of the best things authors can learn is how to *imply*.

Say something... without saying it. We do this all the time in our own speech, but for some reason, we feel our readers need to know every single detail.

I promise you, they don't.

Spelling it out takes the fun out of reading. It leaves nothing to guesswork, which means there's no mystery to pull through the novel. We've already switched to the other POV—we know exactly why Vivian's a badass, and how tragic her backstory is. Which means we got all the drama in a neat little package, contained perfectly in Vivian's POV.

What a wasted opportunity.

A great example of this is *Twilight*. The world devoured that book largely because we wanted to know what the *hell* Edward was. We knew he wasn't human. So what? Stephanie Meyer pulled us through the first fifty pages with a mystery—a mystery that would have been completely ruined if she'd swapped to Edward's POV.

Now, I do think multi-POV can be done well, and I agree it's sometimes necessary. I used dual POV for the first time myself in *Can't Spell Treason Without Tea*. Before that book, I enjoyed the challenge of writing from one character's viewpoint—of telling a story from such a limited perspective.

It was fun to see what I could say without saying it.

In my vast experience editing new authors' work, most books can be written in a single POV... and many of them *should* be.

If you can't make me love your character without shoving me inside their head, that character needs work.

So, challenge yourself! I'm not saying your book shouldn't have multiple points of view—many genres, like fantasy romance, actually sell better with them—but make it an intentional choice.

And if you've never tried writing a book with a single POV, test it out. You might be surprised at how much you enjoy hiding things in plain sight.

FORESHADOWING

Hey, speaking about hiding things in plain sight, let's take a quick pause and discuss foreshadowing.

You remember the example from *Wreck-It Ralph*, back in Chapter 6? Remember how I mentioned King Candy, and how he only surfaced as a villain towards the end?

I think that *Wreck-It Ralph* is one of the greatest examples of foreshadowing, hands-down.

WRECK-IT RALPH

King Candy was our token villain, right? He manifested as an evil-doer—but only in the last 20% of that movie. Before that point, we weren't sure if we could trust him. Normally, a betrayal like King Candy's would have been jarring for viewers—a frustrating twist that didn't really correlate with his personality up to that point.

But we *loved* that twist? Why, you ask?

"You're not going turbo, are you?"

When it's first stated, it's common vernacular. Everyone who hears it *knows* what it means—and because it's said aloud, we don't initially realize it relates to a character. We don't realize it's "going Turbo," not "going turbo."

Not until halfway through the movie, when Ralph's hero, Fix-It Felix Jr., details Turbo's story to another character. That's when we learn what we've already guessed: that Turbo went crazy and game-jumped, taking over another arcade game out of greed.

We knew it meant "game-hopping," but that story added great context.

And more, we'd heard it so many times by that point that it was a *reward* to har that story. We *wanted* the details about Turbo. That's a flashback I couldn't get enough of!

But then, the twist.

But I never, in a million years, imagined Turbo would be King Candy. That this ancient video game villain *never died*. That he actually just rebranded, and continued doing his same old shit.

Fucking. Wow. My jaw dropped when King Candy revealed himself... and all because of that impeccable foreshadowing.

· · ·

WALL-E

Another great example of foreshadowing is *Wall-E*. In a movie with no dialogue for the first half, the visuals do an excellent job of foreshadowing the world we're about to experience. As Wall-E putters through this trash city, we see a single name on the background of every. Single. Image.

Buy N Large.

Without any words at all, we know a massive corporation has overtaken the earth. We know the humans left because of it, on spaceships *funded* by the very corporation that destroyed their planet. We know Wall-E is all that's left—a tiny trash robot, left alone to clean up an insurmountable amount of waste.

We know that Wall-E is going to fix Buy N Large's mess, and we're rooting for him to do it.

FORESHADOWING CAN BE USED for the setting or the plot, but great foreshadowing is *subtle as hell.*

Start to think creatively about how you can weave foreshadowing into your book. Done well, this can be a jaw-dropping moment for your readers!

FILLER WORDS

Here's a list of common filler words, taken from Google.

- Just
- Very
- Stuff
- Actually
- Like
- That
- So
- Literally
- Absolutely
- Then
- Much
- Well
- Even
- Okay
- Always
- But
- Got
- See
- Basically

Most of these don't need to be in your book. As we mentioned in Chapter 6, Round 4 of your edits should be the time to delete them.

This can be tedious, so my suggestion is to identify these words—and **start phasing them out of your writing all**

together. Learn *why* these words are useless or redundant, and avoid them from the beginning.

It's like "um" or "uh" in our everyday speech. They're commonplace, right until the moment you take conscious effort to *stop* saying them.

THE EXCEPTION TO FILLER WORDS:

You may have noticed, but this book is *riddled* with filler words. Clearly, I'm not practicing what I preach here.

Believe it or not, it was a conscious decision. I chose a conversational tone for this craft book, and this is how I speak in real life.

Even in my fiction, I hesitate to delete *all* filler words.

Sometimes, deleting filler words will reduce your writing to robotic drivel, barely better than something an AI could produce.

We're humans. And humans fill the silence with something, even if it doesn't make grammatical sense.

So.

When someone says, "delete filler words," take it with a grain of salt. You know your writing style best. Try to whittle them down if you can, but not at the expense of your true voice.

UTILIZING BODY LANGUAGE

In case you haven't noticed by now, psychology is fascinating to me. The way humans interact seems so unique, and yet almost always follows the same playbook.

Implementing that playbook in your writing will make it better, period. Your characters will feel more real, and your readers will swoon without knowing why.

Therapy has actually helped me a lot with writing solid plots. Most of my characters have excellent communication, because I'd rather find drama in the real issue than a miscommunication. (There are so many reasons for a misunderstanding—and "I just can't tell him right now" is a pretty weak one.)

My job has helped my writing too; I'm a flight attendant, and have ready access to the general public—which lends for a lot of interesting conversations and people watching.

REFERENCE BOOKS on Body Language

In college, I bought a book called ***What Every Body is Saying,*** by Joe Navarro. I adored it, and recommend this book to anyone who wants to elevate their characters' physical actions.

Another great help is ***The Emotion Thesaurus,*** by Angela Ackerman and Becca Puglisi. This book is an essential guide to emotions—and the physical reactions we have while experiencing them.

If your beta reader asks, "Why is everyone always raising their eyebrows?" now might be time to pull out *The Emotion Thesaurus* and hunt for different cues.

Body language has meaning. Crossing your arms is a sign of defense. A slight frown means you're disagreeing silently with what someone says. Angling your foot away from the conversation is a nonverbal cue that you're ready to leave.

Learn these cues—and start weaving them into your story.

AVOID FACIAL CUES

This tip comes directly from Cee M Taylor, a fiction editor and author who posts incredibly helpful videos on TikTok. Back in August 2023, she posted about facial cues—and how authors "shouldn't use them."

Naturally, I reached out to her, because how dare she try to imply that my characters should never smile, wrinkle their noses, narrow their eyes. Those are staples in my writing, damn it.

Her explanation *fascinated* me.

Cee explained that authors fall back on facial cues when there's nothing of interest happening in the background of a conversation. Basically, too much smiling, nose wrinkling, or narrowing eyes is a dead giveaway that there isn't enough tension—or even just ordinary movement—in a scene.

Very rarely are two people talking to each other and doing *nothing* else. Even in the most mundane conversations, someone's checking their phone or fiddling with their clothes—or whatever the fantasy equivalent of that is. Polishing their swords? You get the point.

The example Cee used was an arguing couple. Yeah, they could be debating the future of their relationship, and that has tension. But what if they're debating the future of their relationship

...in a rainstorm

......on the side of the road

.........in a foreign country

............after their car broke down?

Damn.

Immediately, you can see the physical actions that would *replace* your facial cue fallbacks. Instead of smiling, they'll be huffing as they amp the jack. Instead of wrinkling their nose, they'll be hauling a spare tire—and maybe realizing that's flat, too. They might narrow their eyes, but it'll mean more when they're hogging the umbrella while their ex-partner changes a tire during a downpour.

Point is, Cee was right. Facial cues are a crutch for every author, at every experience level. Use them as cues for yourself, instead. If you notice yourself falling back on them—maybe your scene needs a bit of a rework.

FLASHBACKS

In my opinion, there's a right way and a wrong way to do flashbacks.

I don't avoid them entirely, but my rule of thumb is to never, ever let a flashback go longer than two paragraphs. That's right. I don't do entire scene flashbacks.

Why?

Because they're boring.

A flashback is the past—it's already happened. All that scene break accomplishes now is telling, rather than showing, with the added bonus of wrenching your reader violently out of a story they were probably enjoying.

Instead, focus on the impact that event has on your MC's life <u>today</u>.

For example, maybe your MC's mother was murdered. That might seem important to show—the devastation of a little girl, the blood on the floor, the murderer slipping into the night while she watches, terror-stricken, through a cracked cabinet door.

Except I didn't pick up the book to read about your MC as a little girl. I want to read about her badass adult self. I want to know how this event *changed* her.

Instead, show me how her MC's entire life was derailed from that moment. Show me how she triple-locks her doors. Show me the knife under her pillow. Show me her badass private investigator badge, and how her desk is filled with paperwork on a murder long-since closed. And then, when your MC's bestie hisses to a friend, *"Shut up. Her mom died when she was little,"* I suddenly care a lot more.

Brings back that mystery, right?

Flashbacks are another crutch. Sometimes they're necessary, but I challenge you to tell the story without them. If you feel the need, try weaving a flashback into the proper narrative with a tactic like this, from my book *This Gilded Abyss*:

 "Who's visiting?" Nix asked.

"Oh, it's Subarch Kessandra." Leon flashed a wry smile and gestured at the camera. "Find anything good this morning?"

Nix barely heard him. A sudden roaring in her ears drowned him out, and a flash of an unbidden memory: Quian, laughing a little, shoving her shoulder as they lounged in a utilitarian recreation room. *"Kessandra is just a person, Nix. I think you should go for it."*

She shouldn't have listened.

"Sergeant?" Leon asked cautiously.

"The flash of an unbidden memory" is my lead-in to a flashback. Readers know instantly that this is an important memory for my MC, but we only get a taste of it. Just long enough to see how it stalls her in the present day.

Any flashbacks I include are in that format, and they're never long.

If I feel the need to write something more, I always analyze *why*. What's so important about that ancient scene that it needs to come back full force?

Sometimes it's necessary. But most of the time... well. >.>

THOSE ARE MY RANDOM TIPS. Stay tuned for our final chapter —all about diversity, proper representation, and cancel culture.

TWELVE
WRITING DIVERSITY WELL

EARLIER IN THIS BOOK, we asked ourselves the question, **"Why are you the author for this novel?"** Just because we have an idea doesn't mean it's ours to write—or that we're the best author for it.

However, we can't entirely stay in our lane, and that's where this gets complicated.

A DISCLAIMER

Before we dive into this topic: I am a white writer. I'm also ADHD and queer, but I am that basic white bitch drinking pumpkin spice lattes every fall.

I'm speaking on this topic because a book like this would be remiss without it. This is a huge point for writers today, and it's something we need to have continuous discussion around.

But never forget that I'm yet another white voice. When you have the opportunity, please seek out People of Color (PoC) themselves about what kind of rep they'd like to see. They're the authority, not me.

TESTING THE BOUNDARIES OF REPRESENTATION

Back in mid-2022, I was fortunate to witness a massive discussion on BookTok regarding white authors writing diversely. At that time, the general consensus among PoC is that they'd rather see a white-washed book over a book that features poorly represented PoC.

Basically, bad rep is worse than no rep at all.

This is different from 2017 or so, when all I heard was, "you have to add people of color into your books."

Not true these days. If you feel that you *cannot* write diverse characters well, you're better off focusing on your craft, learning from the resource list below, and approaching that topic in the future.

For me specifically, my ecosystem is very diverse. I live in a predominantly white area, but I'm a flight attendant. I travel the country for a living. I've worked many flights where I'm the minority, and my coworkers come from every background imaginable.

White-washing my books feels flat-out wrong to me at this point. That's not my world, so I don't want to portray it in my writing. I really value the inclusivity of my day job, and translating that to fiction is very important to me.

So, if you're nodding along, this section is for you.

POC IN THE PUBLISHING INDUSTRY

Imani (@Imani_the_writer2.0) is a Black BookTokker who's dedicated her platform to resources on writing diversely. In one video from 2021, she spoke about why PoC are fatigued with white writers claiming their stories, displaying them with poor representation—and then getting far more lucrative publishing deals than PoC folk who are trying to write those same stories. *Their* stories.[1]

Let me say that again. White writers are often paid more for writing diverse stories than *diverse writers are.*

If that made you recoil, good. It's fucking horrifying.

Publishing is a predominantly white business. The Big 5 presses are making efforts to diversify their employees and book lists, but the fact is it's happening at a very, very slow rate. Turnover is even higher for PoC than their white counterparts in the publishing industry. And the pay disparity... yikes.

Back in 2020, there was a huge push for transparency in advance rates. Naturally, we cannot share those numbers publicly or our publishers get very, very mad. So an anonymous spreadsheet was created, under the hashtag #PublishingPaidMe.[2]

It was created to raise awareness between the pay disparity of PoC vs. white authors. At the time of creation, 76% of the authors recording deals were white.[3] That number has declined in years since, but it's still not equal to our population.

That spreadsheet is public, by the way. It records a ton of great information, so feel free to check those numbers yourself. (To find this spreadsheet, check the endnote, or google, "#publishingpaidme spreadsheet".)

Point is, this is an age-old discussion, and one that reflects the world at large. It's complex. It's complicated. Just like the cultures you're hoping to represent.

So, let's dive deeper.

THE BIG QUESTION

This is what we're all wondering: How do you include diversity in a novel without impacting your diverse readers negatively?

It's the wrong question to ask. Instead, try this:

> **"Are you writing diverse characters,
> or are you telling diverse *stories*?"**

Our world is varied, so I think it's natural to add diversity into our work. But there is a line between including a diverse cast, and telling a story that isn't yours to tell.

Again, this comes down to your own personal preference, research level, and experiences. If you have grandparents of another culture and spent a lifetime listening to their stories, you might have the learned experience to represent their struggles. If you have a best friend who lives with a specific disability, you likely can portray that disability well in your own fiction, provided your friend helps with the nuances.

However, if you have no ties to a specific type of diverse story, it might not be your wheelhouse.

And that's where we have to be really, really honest with ourselves.

There is no hard and fast answer here. No one is going to come up to you and say, "yes, you can write this, but no, you can't write that." The fact is, no one knows your experiences like you do.

And a lack of clear boundaries is why this terrifies many authors. It's guesswork, like most things in life—but *educated* guesswork is where we need to start.

ESSENTIAL RESOURCES FOR DIVERSE WRITING

Here are some tips for exploring diversity in your writing:

- **Pointedly engage with communities outside your own.** If you live in a predominantly white area, it's time to travel and explore the world at large. Talk to folks of all strokes, and listen to their experiences. (Remember, they are *never* obligated to educate you, but just by having conversations, you'll learn a lot!)

- **Read books about our own internal biases.** We're human, which means we *all* have biases. That central argument, that theme? It's shaped by our own belief systems. Examining your own biases will make you more aware of them inside your fiction.

- **Educate yourself on history.** Examples of oppression, biases, and racial difficulties are everywhere. Misinformation is rampant, so do your best to find authentic, accurate sources of historical events—ideally from those who experienced the oppression firsthand.

- **Actively seek out diverse authors and social media accounts.** Like attracts Like, which means that your FYP is probably not very diverse. Unless you search for diverse booktokkers, bookstagramers, facebook groups, etc, you likely won't ever see them. Especially on TikTok, great conversations about diversity in writing are happening, directly from the mouths of those who suffer from poor representation. Listen to them, learn from them. (*Hint*: if you're unsure how to find these social media accounts, put out a call. Simply say, "I'm looking for diverse [insert platform here] accounts. Who do you enjoy following?" Authors love to share their favorite influencers!)

- **Bookmark the "Writing with Color" blog.** This is an older Tumblr blog from the early '10s, but it's still one of my favorite resources. It's a huge collection of articles about writing diversely, written from folk of those backgrounds. It's fabulous. (URL: https://writingwithcolor. tumblr.com/)
- **When in doubt, hire sensitivity readers.** A sensitivity reader is someone of that background who explores a book with diverse characters and analyzes your representation. They're literally hired to find problems before the general public does, so they're invaluable to authors!

A Note on Sensitivity Readers:

Sensitivity readers range in cost depending on their exclusivity. For example, I've hired Black sensitivity readers for around $300, but paid almost $1000 for a Japanese one.

(I was told this is because Japanese culture has a heavy emphasis on being polite, so telling someone when they're promoting harmful rep goes against their baseline. It takes a very special skillset, which is why there aren't many Japanese sensitivity readers out there.)

If you're self-publishing, these readers can be an incredibly helpful asset if you're worried about the representation in your book. I highly recommend budgeting for one.

If you're going the traditional publishing route, it's possible your publisher might hire a sensitivity reader for you, which is great! But not all of them will bother with this—check with your literary agent to explore options.

SUMMARY - WRITING DIVERSELY

Point is, there are a lot of ways to expand your worldviews—but it takes time and effort on your part. That's what folks are expecting from their authors these days—and rightly so.

Authors will spend hours exploring the history of the sundial or researching how submarines work. Why wouldn't we spend at least that much time and energy examining the nuances of another culture?

Write your book with the best, educated intentions, and if it still doesn't hit home with your audience—well, continue reading.

THE CANCEL CULTURE SECTION

We've already talked about diversity, inclusion, and whether or not *you* are the author for your story.

The unfortunate fact is that sometimes, you aren't—and if that's the case, your readers will let you know. Loudly.

Every author's nightmare, I'm sure.

I'll preface that this section addresses a perfect scenario. One where you don't have a backlist of abuse / bullying / bad representation, one where your readers are willing to default to grace and education over pitchforks.

Sometimes, it doesn't happen that way. Sometimes, social media takes a topic and runs.

I just think that's the horror story, not the default.

In my experience watching *and* living this, indignation doesn't happen in a vacuum. There seems to be a flow to an author being corrected for poor representation.

1. A reader finds a problem—a bad theme, poor representation, etc.
2. Reader voices the problem, and it catches steam on social media.
3. Readers demand accountability from the author.
4. The author responds.
5. Depending on response, the issue either dies... or blows up.

The important thing to note:

The author almost always has an opportunity, even a brief one, to respond.

Back in the late 00's, early '10s, when social media really started exploding, this backlash became such a problem that publishers started sneaking clauses into their contracts to protect themselves. They're called "moral clauses," and the Author's Guild has a scathing statement against them.[4] (Read it here: https://authorsguild.org/news/why-we-oppose-morals-clauses-in-book-contracts/)

It's a serious issue... but it's nearly impossible to avoid some kind of reader backlash.

Today, authors are encouraged to be present in online spaces. We're conducting interviews. We're interacting with fans on a very personal level. All that conversation? Something's bound to go wrong, regardless of intention.

So, let's prepare for that moment.

WHY ARE BOOKS / AUTHORS CANCELED?

When something ignites, authors who are paying attention can fix the problem early. And how genuine our apology is—how sincere our actions are to *fix* the issue— seems to directly correlate with how big the fire grows.

I believe most flames can be extinguished at the candle size, if you're smart enough to *listen* to your readers. Social media is volatile, but **readers rarely get outraged for no reason.**

They're outraged because *someone was hurt.*

Whether the author intended it or not, a marginalized group was harmed. An author said or wrote something that might have worked in the past, but is absolutely tone-deaf today. And since new generations are, as a whole, trying to make the world a more inclusive place… they spoke up.

This is *good*. This is personally the direction I want my readers to take, and I hope you do too.

Nice thing is, in my experience, **most readers recognize that authors are human and make mistakes.**

Very rarely does an author start a book with intention to harm. We don't wake up with this evil villain mindset. We just didn't know better.

Authors usually mean the best, which means *this* is a fantastic opportunity to explore a sincere, authentic response, and educate yourself in the process.

BEFORE YOU RESPOND, TAKE A BREATH.

Anger is linked to judgment within our own minds. If someone threatens the image we have of ourselves—the thought that "I'm a good person," or "I'm always inclusive,"—our natural instinct is to lash back.

When someone says, "This wasn't cool," our monkey-brains retort, "Well, what do you know?"

Slap the monkey brain. That defensive mindset won't get you anywhere in life, even if it's automatic for every single brain on the planet.

Before we dive into the fix for cancel culture, let me reiterate.

You *are* still a good person.
You *are* trying to be inclusive.
You just made a mistake. And that's okay.

This is a learning opportunity, and a moment to become closer with your readers. It's not an attack on you, even if it's presented that way.

It's a chance to become a better version of yourself.

Fantastic. :D

Now. Let's talk about next steps.

THE LAST METHOD

Someone was harmed by your words. It's your job to fix it. Here's what you're going to do—taken directly from my decade as a flight attendant.

LAST.
Listen. Apologize. Solve. Thank.

It's the very basis of all great customer service—and that's what you're offering here. You're an author with a product, and your readers are your customers. Time to address their concerns.

FIRST: BE QUIET AND *LISTEN.*

Social media has a way of inciting all the wrong emotions. But anyone in customer service knows that when someone is yelling at you, *everything gets worse if you yell back.*

If you want to de-escalate a situation, calmly and quietly listen to what they're saying. If I've learned one thing on Booktok and Bookstagram, it's that these readers are incredibly articulate.

When they raise concerns, there's a *reason.*

So. Put the phone down. Find a trusted friend to vent. Let your emotions boil... and then ease into a simmer, then quiet all together. And when you feel calmer, that's the moment to consider that maybe, these people have a point.

A lot of authors say, "Is my career worth dying on this hill?"

I say, "Why would you *want* to exclude a certain group from enjoying your books?"

Whatever your stance, listening is the first step. Please. **Stop talking** and pay attention.

SECOND: APOLOGIZE SINCERELY, WITH THE WORDS, "I'M SORRY."

You can't stay silent forever. In situations like this, there's a pause. Readers voiced a concern, and then they'll wait to see if the author responds.

If silence is the answer, it speaks louder than words.

Your next step is to apologize.

Maya Angelou said, "People will forget what you said, people will forget what you did, but people will never forget how you made them feel."

Remember that. Good intentions mean nothing now. It doesn't matter what you *meant* to convey with that passage, or that character, or that theme.

You harmed a group of people,
and that needs addressing.

But first, let's take another breath.

It's *okay*.

It's **okay** that you made a mistake. You are not a bad person. You are not evil. You are human—and trust me, we have *all* been there. I have personally made so, so many of these missteps. I'm sure in this book alone, I'll get emails about some insensitive passage or poorly chosen word, and need to upload a new version to Amazon.

I'm human. You're human. Don't judge yourself, and don't lash out at the group raising awareness.

Just do better next time.

With that nonjudgmental mindset, swallow your anger—and formulate an apology. If you're confused about why this is happening, tell your readers you're taking this seriously and will have an actionable response in a few days. Spend that time investigating everything about this issue, ideally from the diverse voices raising concerns. I know you've researched already, but clearly, it wasn't enough.

While you address your readers, say the words, "I'm sorry."

Do not tiptoe around that phrase. Physically say "I'm sorry"—and *mean* it. (If you don't mean your apology yet, that's okay. Emotions might still be heightened. Back up to the Listen step, and do some more introspection. You'll get there!)

When you're done apologizing, finish with, "I made a mistake, but I promise: I hear you, and I'm going to fix this."

THIRD: SOLVE THE PROBLEM.

This is the moment where most authors go wrong. It's one thing to offer lip service—apologizing and pretending to mean it. But if you don't *fix* the problem, you're essentially admitting that there's no problem to fix.

Clearly, that is incorrect, or you wouldn't be at this step.

Take this seriously, and think hard about a *good* fix. The steps you take typically need to correlate with the size of the fire.

That 2022 debate on BookTok was kicked off for a white writer offering poor Black representation. Her response was to fix the issue, but then offer the original version as a "special" first edition.

Y i k e s.

Use your common sense, is what I'm saying. And if it doesn't seem common to you, consult with some trusted friends who know this industry. A literary agent, maybe, or your publisher, or another established author.

To be honest, this is the most satisfying step for me. Fixing the issue. Resolving the conflict. I've apologized, and now it's time to buckle down and figure out how to rectify my mistake.

The good news is, some sensitivity issues are portrayed in just a few lines: a character acts too violent in one scene, or a word linked to another meaning without proper context, or a description goes awry. Those are easy to fix!

THE BAGEL EXAMPLE:

My biggest sensitivity issue was the bagel incident of *Can't Spell Treason Without Tea*. One of my characters made fresh bagels, and it was a new food for their world. I added it simply because I love bagels!

But I wasn't aware that bagels were created by Jewish folk during WWII after they were banned from baking bread.

Obviously, the casual use of such an important, historic food—from a culture I don't represent—was problematic. But I had no idea until I read a few reviews and saw that people were uneasy.

Once I became aware of the problem, I fixed it. I removed any mention of bagels from the edited version of that book, and replaced them with kolaches, which are from my own cultural background.

This fix was a bit delayed because my publisher was involved at this point. If it were just my original, self-published book, I'd have made the changes and uploaded a new version to Amazon. Easy! But because a publisher had already taken control of online sales, I had to leave the old version up until republication of the paperback—when the edits would sync across all versions.

Still, my fans are aware that I've addressed the issue, and now it's out of my hands. I apologized, and the bagels are gone from future editions.

And you know what? I learned something! That's my favorite part of this process; understanding where I made a mistake so I can avoid it later.

After all, I'm only human. This kind of thing makes me feel like I can be a better version of myself someday. :)

Fixing Plot Issues

Now, there may be a more complex issue if the problem is the plot. If you incorporated a theme or event that wasn't yours to pull from—something that will drastically change the story if you try to alter it—that will complicate things. *Especially* if you have a publisher who's already bought the book.

In that case, you may need to work hand-in-hand with your publisher to resolve the issue. They don't want this kind of backlash either, so they'll likely be excited for a fresh rewrite to fix things. And if they aren't... that's when you get your literary agent involved.

As a self-published author, you have more freedom to fix this problem. You control your release date, and whether or not your book is live for purchase. If something huge is impacting it, *take the book down.* Tell your readers you're working on revisions, hire some sensitivity readers to ensure it's done well, and then relaunch the book at a later date.

But ideally, we'll avoid those big, sweeping edits anyway, because we've already done the hard work to examine our internal biases.

The easiest time to fix a plot or theme is *before* you write the book, so always remember to run your ideas by a few trusted friends first!

FOURTH: THANK YOUR READERS FOR THEIR TIME.

"Thank them for *their* time? They just created a problem that cause *me* to lose time!"

No, they didn't. You caused harm. They brought attention to that issue. Believe it or not, marginalized folk are *not* required to spend their day educating people outside their communities. But they do spend that time, because it's important.

I'm always so grateful to have readers like this. This job is my dream. I want to be the best author I can be, because it's what I've been imagining since I was a teenager.

Every time a sensitivity issue is raised with one of my books—and there have been several, trust me—I'm flooded with gratitude that these readers took the time out of their day to *tell* me about the problem.

How lucky are we that we get the chance to share our stories with the world? Some stories may not land, but each one gets better than the last—and it's largely because of the time these communities take to help us authors understand their perspectives.

We can't know everything outside of our own community. We can't possibly understand what it's like to be someone else—but that's the job we signed up for. So, every time you get the chance to test out the LAST method, that's a moment where you become *better* at your passion.

And I think that's pretty damn great!

Aim for gratitude over anger, folks. It'll get you so much further, and make you so many more friends.

CURATING A SAFE SPACE

This is something I don't see talked about very often, but it's honestly been such an eye-opener for me.

Just by voicing my interest in learning about diverse issues, I've created a safe space for my readers.

Anyone who follows me on TikTok knows I'm open to learning and growing as a person. Because I reiterate this any chance I get, my readers have slated me as someone who will offer a safe space for constructive feedback.

That means they usually come to me *privately* with issues, rather than voicing them on social media.

Not always, of course. Some readers have no interest in emailing me. But my ARC readers are told explicitly that they can email me anytime with sensitivity concerns. I try to find beta readers from all backgrounds and cultures for that reason. I hire sensitivity readers.

It's important to me that my rep is solid, and my readers usually know it.

Curate a safe space where readers can approach you with concerns. If you are open about welcoming sensitivity feedback, everything gets easier.

And if things do heat up for you at some point, just take a breath and re-read this section. You're a good person. Fix the issue, and apologize for the harm.

You've got this!

THIRTEEN

THE END

HEYYY, we made it! That wasn't too bad, was it?

... Was it?

Well, I'm going to assume you had a great time, and are primed to start writing your novel! Working on a book is one of my greatest joys, and I hope this gave you the courage to finally finish that book you've had in mind.

The scariest part of writing is starting, after all!

In the meantime, remember that you have examples of great fiction all around you. Every great writer was built on the books that came before, so take some conscious effort to explore your favorites. Movies, games, TV shows, books... whatever floats your boat!

Whenever I'm consuming fiction and something really hits home, I actually stop reading and start analyzing. I'll

wipe the tears off my face, whisper a congratulations to the author, and reread what incited the emotion. How did the author make me *feel* this way? What techniques did they utilize in their book—was it character related? Structural? Sentence-level?

And then, I mimic it.

That's right. I blatantly try to copy the techniques that move me emotionally. As a writer, I'm constantly exploring my writing style. I can nail it down to a few descriptors—witty banter, fast-paced action, easily digestible—but that style only came about because I explored others. Ally Carter. Tamora Pierce. Jane Austen. Any book that turns my head, I start analyzing their writing style.

Over time, I was able to define my own quite neatly. It just took practice and an intelligent approach to reading.

If you're new to writing, this might seem intimidating, but over time it becomes second nature. You already know what an Inciting Incident is—can you find it in your TBR books? I bet you'll see it instantly, now that you know what you're looking for.

Either way, you are killing it. You're the 6% that's actually going to Do The Thing. Everyone else in the world just *thinks* about doing it. You're over here ready to finish, and then publish it!

Basically, you're kicking ass.

Get out there and make the world a better place. We need your story!!

RESOURCES

This book was short as hell (about 39,000 words, if you're curious), and it's because so many other craft writers have said this stuff better than me. If you're looking for more writing help, you can't get better than the books on this list.

I've organized them in the way I feel is most helpful. Start at the top, work your way down! Or skip around to what sounds interesting; they're all worth a read.

Craft Books

First 50 Pages - Jeff Gerke

- A fantastic analysis into perfecting your opening pages. This book explores everything from setting up stakes to identifying character flaws and everything in between. An *essential* writing guide on your first 50 pages!

Plot vs Character - Jeff Gerke

- Yet another classic, in my mind. This book dives into what's more important—plot or character—and how to make them both shine.

My Story Can Beat Up Your Story - Jeffery Schechter

- My absolute favorite guide on plotting. The graph Jeffery Schechter includes in this book was invaluable to understanding plot structure.
- NOTE: I personally don't feel this book is as helpful past the halfway point. It gets technical in the same way *Save the Cat* does. Feel free to stop reading if it overwhelms!

Writing Magic - Gail Carson Levine

- This book is aimed at children, but is one of my all-time favorites. It's super short, so you can finish it in an hour or so. A great overview from a legendary author about how to write a book.
- (This one's a perfect gift for any budding authors in your family, too!)

7 Figure Fiction - T Taylor

- A hidden GEM of a book. **Buy this one. Now.**
- This book addresses the common dreams all readers share—sometimes overlapping with our favorite tropes, but not always—and narrows down how to use them in your fiction to make your books irresistible.

Romancing the Beat - Gwen Hayes

- Our absolute classic for writing romance. Romance books are *very* formulaic, and Gwen Hayes breaks that formula perfectly.
- Very short read, absolutely worth it.

Wired for Story - Lisa Cron

- Another staple for the discerning writer. This book identifies psychological tricks to hack your reader's brain and make them adore your novel.
- (It was a bit theme-heavy for me, but I still think it's worth your time!)

Save the Cat - Blake Snyder

- A classic that I'm adding simply because it's a classic. There's useful tips in here, but I wrote this book because *Save the Cat*'s craft approach is... in-depth.
- Perfect for plotters. Anxiety central for pantsers and plantsers.

- Still, worth a read if you haven't yet... if just to join conversations about it!

Save the Cat Writes a Novel - Jessica Brody

- The novel alternative for *Save the Cat*. There's a ton of overlap between books and screenplays, but if you want one specifically for writing books, this is it.

What Every BODY is Saying - Joe Navarro

- Not a craft book, but still an excellent resource for writers! This book details body language—and the subtle cues we all use to indicate our desires and emotions.

Story Trumps Structure - Steven James

- Another analysis of plot structure. I liked this one a lot, although I don't think it's more useful for "Eureka!" moments than *My Story Can Beat Up Your Story*.
- Again, worth a read if you've chewed through this list and crave more!

How to Write a Novel Using the Snowflake Method - Randy Ingermanson

How to Write a Dynamite Scene Using the Snowflake Method - Randy Ingermanson

- These books by Randy Ingermanson weren't quite my cup of tea, but that's likely because the Snowflake Method is too in-depth for me. Still, these books are very well-rated, and might be a solid option for anyone who wants more than this book provided!

Structuring Your Novel - K.M. Weiland

Outlining Your Novel - K.M. Weiland

- Both of these books by K.M. Weiland are great analysis into outlining and structuring your books! Again, no lightbulb moments for me, but a lot of great tips woven throughout.

Get a Literary Agent - Chuck Sambuchino*

- A comprehensive overview of the publishing industry, and actionable how-tos on querying literary agents, and what to expect during that process.
- NOTE: This book was written in 2014, and the publishing landscape changes fast. The pandemic changed a *lot.* Keep in mind some of the content may be outdated!

WEBSITE RESOURCES

Writing with Color - https://writingwithcolor.tumblr.com/

- The absolute essential reference guide to writing diversely. Written by a collection of diverse authors over the '10s, this blog hosts many staple articles about diversity and avoiding harmful representation.

Jane Friedman - https://janefriedman.com/

- A long-standing presence in the industry, Jane Friedman's blog offers insights into writing and the ever-changing landscape of publishing.

The Author's Guild - https://authorsguild.org/

- This is confusing, as there is a WRITER'S Guild, and an AUTHOR'S Guild. Both are very helpful resources, but the Author's Guild offers a great, in-depth analysis of proper publishing contracts and statements on current events.
- This is a great resource for any author hoping to have legal protections when negotiating contracts. They offer free contract consultations to members.

Publisher's Weekly - https://www.publishersweekly.com/

- This is how I get most of my publishing information. Publisher's Weekly offers a daily snapshot of current events in the publishing industry, sent via email. If you're curious about events shaping authors and writing spaces, subscribe here!

Pub Rants - https://nelsonagency.com/pub-rants/

- This is one of the longest-standing literary agent blogs out there, and arguably one of the most helpful. Agent Kristin Nelson began this blog in (I think?) 2005, and finally threw in the towel in 2022. But over that period, she wrote *so many* helpful articles on writing and publishing.
- NOTE: Some of this content is also outdated. Make sure you check the date of the publishing advice before taking it to heart—some things from 2005 - 2015 no longer apply. If you're unsure, check with an actively querying (or recently represented) author for what's factual nowadays.

Writer Beware - https://writerbeware.blog/

- The final resource here is Writer Beware, which is a necessity for both traditional and self-publishing. The minute an author enters the scene with intent to publish, they'll face scam artists trying to take their intellectual property.

- Protect yourself by reviewing this website often. **If something seems too good to be true, it probably is.**

MY FAVORITE DIVERSE TikTokkers

Looking for people to follow? Here's my *bare-bones* starter list of accounts. (Making lists terrifies me, because I always know I'm leaving someone important out—and I'll kick myself for it later. If that's you, please know that I still love you and just panicked while making this list. LOL.)

It's primarily focused on PoC, but with a few ND and LGBTQIA+ creators as well!

(If you aren't on TikTok, several of these folk have other social media platforms too! There are amazing, diverse folk on every platform!)

MUST-FOLLOW TikTok ACCOUNTS:

- Satrayreads - @satrayreads
- Imani - @imani_the_writer2.0
- Owl Your Librarian - @owlslibrary98
- Lee | Booktok - @books.with.lee
- Niah - @novelniah

- Mari - @mynameismarines
- Torri - @blackromanceconnoisseur
- Moss SensitivityReader - @mossnightwing
- Michael LaBorn - @Michael.laborn
- October K, Author - @okwrites
- Emily Sarah - @emilysarahart
- Little District Books - @littledistrictbooks
- Ruthie Bowles Narrator - @ruthie.narrates.books
- Sammie - @booksdogsandcoffee
- Katrina's Library - @katrinaslibrary
- Melissa Blair - @melissas.bookshelf
- Natalia Hernandez - @nataliahernandezauthor
- Hidithescribe - @hidithescribe
- Sim booktoks badly - @simkern
- Schizophrenicreads Nathan - @schizophrenicreads
- Chrissy - @chrissymarshall_
- TheHarperMcKenzie - @theharpermckenzie
- Crab and Bell - BookTok - @crabandbell

As a reminder, if you're ever unsure about how to find diverse accounts on your preferred social media platform, you can always put out a call! Authors *love* sharing their favorite accounts, and will typically tag several amazing creators. :)

Don't ever be afraid to ask for help!

NOTES

1. SO, YOU WANT TO WRITE A BOOK?

1. Melore, Chris. "More than Half of Americans Think Their Life Is Worthy of a Book Deal." Study Finds, 7 Feb. 2023, studyfinds.org/writing-books-life-worthy-of-deal/.

3. MY INSPIRATION FOR THE 5 SENTENCE METHOD

1. Moore, Mary Carroll. "Word Count Goals for the Three Acts of Your Novel, Memoir, or Nonfiction Book." *How to Plan, Write, and Develop a Book*, 18 Feb. 2022, howtoplanwriteanddevelopabook.blogspot.com/2022/02/word-count-goals-for-three-acts-of-your.html.
2. "The Snowflake Method for Designing a Novel." *Advanced Fiction Writing*, 12 Mar. 2022, www.advancedfictionwriting.com/articles/snowflake-method/.

4. THE 5 SENTENCE METHOD

1. Gerke, Jeff. *The First 50 Pages: Engage Agents, Editors, and Readers, and Set up Your Novel for Success.* Writer's Digest Books, 2011.

12. WRITING DIVERSITY WELL

1. Imani. "Make Your Day." *TikTok*, 22 May 2021, www.tiktok.com/t/ZT8H1ddFf.
2. "#PUBLISHINGPAIDME." *Google Sheets*, Google, docs.google.com/spreadsheets/d/1Xsx6rKJtafa8f_prlYYD3zRxaXYVDaPXbasvt_i-A2vA/edit#gid=1798364047. Accessed 18 Dec. 2023.

3. Adrigold. "[Discussion] #Publishingpaidme Spreadsheet." *Reddit*, 1 Aug. 2022, www.reddit.com/r/PubTips/comments/wdqiqy/comment/iikqlml/?utm_source=share&utm_medium=web2x&context=3.

4. "Why We Oppose Morals Clauses in Book Contracts." *The Authors Guild*, 24 Jan. 2019, authorsguild.org/news/why-we-oppose-morals-clauses-in-book-contracts/.

ACKNOWLEDGMENTS

Did I mention I have a fear of lists?

It comes full force in the acknowledgements, because I know—I *know*—I'll forget someone great, and then feel like shit about it.

So, I'm trying to keep these short. >.>

I always wanted to write a craft book, but never felt like I had useful things to say—or that I could say these things better than other authors have already. But when multiple videos about the 5 Sentence Method topped 100k views each, I finally took the hint.

So, thank you to everyone who watched those videos, and a special thank-you to everyone who left comments or stitched / tagged me after you got this method working. I would never have had the courage to write this book without you!

As always, thanks to my family and friends, who are eternally patient when I claim I'm going to "take a month" and "relax," and then dive into writing a craft book "for fun."

A special thank-you to my beta readers: Samantha Griffis, Alexis Night, Chris Bell, and Amy Nevills. As soon as I get the physical author copies, your signed version is on its way!

(A bonus thanks to the 100+ folks who applied to be a beta reader in a mere 24 hours. That was so encouraging!!)

Huge thanks to Amphi (https://www.books-amphi.studio/) for your incredible help with all my covers—even the ridiculous ones like this. And another thanks to @ohjeezoman for her perpetual flow of adorable dragons in silly positions.

Finally, a thanks to YOU, for picking up this book and giving it a shot.

Teaching writing is my lifelong passion, and I'm so happy to have this chance. You make my dream possible; thank you so, so much!

ABOUT THE AUTHOR

Rebecca Thorne is an author of all things fantasy, sci-fi, and sapphic romance. She thrives on deadlines, averages 2,700 words a day, and tries to write at least 2 books a year. (She also might be a little hyper-focused ADHD.)

When she's not writing (or avoiding writing), Rebecca can be found traveling the country as a flight attendant, or doing her best impression of a granola-girl hermit with her dogs.

Check out Rebecca's website: http://rebeccathorne.net/

facebook.com/rebeccathornewrites

instagram.com/rebeccathornewrites

tiktok.com/@rebecca.thorne

ALSO BY REBECCA THORNE

COZY FANTASIES

Can't Spell Treason Without Tea

A Pirate's Life for Tea

Book 3 - Expected Fall 2024

Book 4 - Expected Winter 2025

FANTASY THRILLERS

This Gilded Abyss

Book 2 - Expected Spring 2024

Book 3 - Expected Summer 2025

CONTEMPORARY FANTASIES

The Day Death Stopped

MIDDLE GRADE

The Secrets of Star Whales